Susan Bulanda

Boston Terriers

Everything About Selection, Care, Nutrition, Behavior, and Training

BARRON'S

2 CONTENTS

UNDERSTANDING THE BOSTON TERRIER

The Boston Terrier was developed in 1865 by a handful of coachmen living in the Beacon Hill area of Boston. They used their employers' purebred dogs as foundation stock to create a unique new breed. Instead of becoming a fighting dog, the ladies of Boston fell in love with the cute Boston Terrier, and it became a popular house dog.

History of the Breed

The Boston Terrier was developed by crossing the Old English Toy Bulldog with the white English Terrier, and adding in a bit of French Bulldog. Through inbreeding, mutations, and accidents, the Boston Terrier was shaped into what it is today.

The Old English Toy Bulldog was similar to the Boston Terrier but the breed tended to be small, and in the nineteenth century it was considered to have no useful purpose. Toy Bulldogs had a following in France, and most were exported there rather than to the United States.

It is said that the Boston Terrier was created out of curiosity—to see what could be developed—and, perhaps, to produce a new fighting dog. But it never gained popularity as a fighter. Instead, it later became popular with women as a pet.

The early Boston Terriers did not look anything like today's version, and the original Beacon Hill breeders would not at all appreciate what they would see today. Most likely, they would consider the modern breed to be much too fine and effeminate. The original Boston Terrier was developed as a "man's" dog. It was not bred for markings or color but rather for its small size.

During the nineteenth century it was common practice to prefix a dog's personal name with the last name of its owner. Thus, the ancestor of all modern Boston Terriers was a dog known as Hooper's Judge. Judge lived during the 1860s and was owned by Mr. Robert C. Hooper of Boston. Mr. Hooper purchased Judge from Mr. William O'Brien, who had imported the dog from Europe.

Hooper's Judge was a cross between an English Bulldog and an English Terrier, with

═BOSTON PERSONALS═

Sam Anderson says, "Orca has me trained. When 5:00 P.M. arrives, he comes to the office and gets me to go downstairs to watch the news and get his toys and play.

"Orca has a bed downstairs and in the office. If his special towel is in the dryer, he will go to the dryer, pull the towel out, and drag it to his bed. Then he will cover himself completely before going to sleep. Orca once fell out of a blanket that was going into the washing machine.

"Orca loves his ball so much that he will carry it home for two to three miles. He goes to the top of hills to roll his ball down so that he can chase it.

"He knows each of his toys by name.

"When I am not feeling well, Orca always cheers me up with a kiss.

"Orca loves to fly. When he finishes his Freestyle performance or if he wants to get away from something, he will fly into my arms. He loves to Lure Course and even beats the Whippets!

"Orca runs to the mail truck when the mail is being delivered because his mail-person always gives him a bone. He likes to jump into the truck and find it. One mailman did not find it funny when Orca jumped into the mail truck and started going through the mail. Now Orca makes sure it is 'his' mailperson first before he jumps into the truck.

"When Orca hears the electric toothbrush in the morning, he jumps onto the toilet seat to get his teeth brushed. He loves poultry-flavored toothpaste."

looks that favored the Bulldog. The English Bulldogs of that period did not resemble the breed of today, but rather the modern American Staffordshire Terrier. Judge was dark brindle with a white stripe through his face and weighed about 32 pounds (14.5 kg).

According to some reports, Judge's breeder was Mr. R. M. Higginson. His sire is said to have been a dog named Langdon's Crib, whose sire in turn was Nevin's Steel. Both Crib and Steel were said to be Bulldogs. Judge was bred to a white female named Gyp or Kate. She weighed about 20 pounds (9 kg) and was owned by Mr. Edward Burnett of Southboro. Gyp was well built and had a three-quarter tail. Records do not show any additional matings for Hooper's Judge, so we can only wonder what became of him.

Inbreeding was subsequently carried out for a number of generations. Other imported bloodlines were then introduced into the strain. One of these was the Scottish Perry, a dog of about 6 pounds (2.7 kg) with a straight three-quarter tail. Another, the Jack Reed, was an evenly marked, rough-coated, reddish brindle-and-white animal, weighing 12 to 14 pounds (5.4–6.4 kg), and carrying a straight three-quarter tail.

Yet another import was Kelly's Brick, a fierce dog weighing about 16 pounds (7.3 kg). He was white with black spots, had a large skull and large eyes, and, once again, a straight tail. There was also O'Brien's Ben, who was short and cobby, with a white-and-brindle coat, weighing about 20 pounds (9 kg), and also with a straight three-quarter-length tail.

The inbreeding then continued, producing Well's Eph and Tobin's Kate. From the breeding of Eph and Kate came Barnard's Tom and Atkinson's Toby. Tom and Toby were important

foundations as sires for the breed. Tom had a cobby body and is credited with being the first Boston with a screw tail. This type of tail was first regarded as a deformity, but it was later established as a legitimate trait when it was traced back to a white English Bulldog female named Fancy (whelped between 1840 and 1850). From these dogs came Summerville Countess, Princess Queen (1891), and Nancy III (1896). Tom and Toby were great dogs, and it is generally agreed that the females sired by them produced the most highly regarded offspring of the period.

Tom's owner, Mr. John P. Barnard, who maintained a kennel of Bulldogs and Bull Terriers, thoroughly enjoyed his new animals. The new cross went by several names: Round-headed Bull and Terrier, Bullethead, and American Bull Terrier.

The first Boston Terriers met with quite a bit of opposition from dog fanciers, as neither the Bull Terrier proponents nor the Bulldog fanciers would accept the new breed. If Boston Terriers were allowed at dog shows at all, they were given a separate class. In these early years the competition between the various dog clubs became nasty. At one point, the Boston Terrier fanciers launched a press campaign that attempted to portray the Bulldog as a savage animal unfit for gentle society. Bulldog fanciers retaliated with claims that the Boston Terrier was nothing more than a mongrel.

In 1889, after some 19 years of development, about 30 fanciers in and around Boston

has leveled off. The popularity of the Boston Terrier is not limited to the United States, but has spread throughout the world.

Some of the earliest Boston Terriers to be recognized by the American Kennel Club were:
- ✔ Hector, whelped 1891, brindle and white
- ✔ Dixie, whelped 1891
- ✔ Punch, whelped 1888, fawn and white
- ✔ Mike, whelped 1893, brindle and white

The first champion of breed was a dog named Topsy, whose registration had originally been canceled due to impure breeding.

Some of the early kennel names were: Albert Alward's Donnybrook, Edward Axtell's St. Botolphs, J. P. Barnard's Myrtle Street, F. G. Bixby's Bixbys, W. L. Davis's Willowbrook, G. B. Doyle's Doyles, A. L. Goode's Goodes, W. C. Hook's Somerville, W. G. Kendall's Squantum, F. A. Locks's Bayonne, P. McDonald's Shawmut, J. Vardum Mott's Presto, A. T. Mount's Oakmount, Myron W. Robinson's Rob

formed the American Bull Terrier Club and exhibited their dogs, which were called Round Heads or Bull Terriers, at local dog shows. The new club met with quite a bit of opposition from Bull Terrier breeders, as well as from the American Kennel Club, which did not want to recognize the Boston Terrier breed.

About two years later, in 1891, the club was renamed the Boston Terrier Club of America, and the name of the breed was changed to the Boston Terrier.

The bickering between the clubs continued until 1893, when the Boston Terrier was officially recognized by the American Kennel Club. After that, everyone buried the hatchet, for the most part, and became friends.

By the 1920s the Boston Terrier became so popular that the breed may well have accounted for 20 to 30 percent of dog show entries of that decade. Since that time interest

BOSTON PERSONALS

Myrt Horn says, "Tinkerbell loves to play in the water bowl, so you cannot fill it up or she will spill it all over the floor. She also 'kills' the vacuum cleaner and the lawn mower by chasing them. When I was ill, Tinkerbell climbed up the bedspread onto my bed and would not leave my side. She would have a fit if anyone tried to lock her out of my room.

"Tinkerbell loves to watch animal shows on TV and will kiss the animals on the TV screen."

Roy, G. A. Rawson's Druid, W. E. Stone's Stones, and C. F. Sullivan's Trimount.

As previously mentioned, often a dog's personal name was preceded by the owner's. Hooper's Judge, for example, indicates that the dog's name was Judge and the owner's name was Hooper. By the same token, the first part of the kennel's name frequently reflects the name of the kennel's owner—such as W. E. Stone, the owner of the kennel named "Stones." This information is important when you study pedigrees, since it helps you to identify the lines in your dog's ancestry. The study of dogs' pedigrees can reveal many interesting stories about people and their dogs.

Note: Boston Terriers are so cute and lovable that the reader of this book might at some point consider breeding Boston Terriers. Before you consider doing this, the author wishes to urge you to carefully research what is involved with established breeders. Because the Boston Terrier is not a breed of dog that is easy to reproduce, breeding should be done only by professionals who are experienced or with the help of an experienced breeder. Boston Terriers as a rule have very small litters and must be born by cesarean section. Once the puppies are born, they can have difficulty breathing and nursing. Therefore, there are few breeders that actually make a profit breeding Boston Terriers.

Nature of the Boston Terrier

Notwithstanding the descent of the modern Boston Terrier from fighting dogs, the character of the breed is such that it is often called the "American Gentleman." Although Bostons are not scrappers, true to their terrier nature they are able to take care of themselves when threatened. They have gentle dispositions, and make excellent house dogs and companions. Boston Terriers are gentle with children and very affectionate with their families. They are an intelligent breed, and are very alert. They make good watchdogs for the home, and are quick to alert the family to anything amiss.

The Boston Terrier has a unique sense of humor, and generally loves to play. It would not be unusual for a Boston to size up a visitor in your home, decide that he or she is a good prospect for a game, and then run to get his favorite toy for some "throw and fetch." They are active dogs that would rather take part in family activities than be left alone. Boston Terriers are not barkers. They tend to live to 10 to 13 years of age.

As a Companion

Because they are affectionate and fun to have around, Boston Terriers make lively, amusing companions. Since they are small, friendly dogs, people want to pet and play with them. The Boston Terrier's social nature, fun-loving spirit, and warm, soft eyes can entice into interacting those people who would not play with other dogs.

But even if your dog's sole purpose in life is to keep you company, your Boston Terrier

CHECKLIST

Activities for Your Boston Terrier
Obedience Competition
Canine Freestyle
Rally-Style Obedience
Agility
Flyball
DiscDog Competition
Canine Good Citizen Award
Therapy Dog

should be given basic obedience training to ensure that he becomes a well-behaved dog that will be a welcome guest in any home. Any dog can be either a joy or a nuisance, depending upon how well you take care of him and how well he has learned his manners.

Sports and Activities for Your Boston Terrier

There are a number of organized activities in which you and your Boston terrier can participate, both for fun and competition.

If you wish to learn about showing your dog in conformation shows, read *The Complete Guide to Showing Your Dog* by Cheryl S. Smith and published by Prima Publishing.

If you wish to learn about the organizations listed under Information you can find them by doing a search on the Internet or by calling the American Kennel Club or United Kennel Club.

IS THIS THE RIGHT BREED FOR YOU?

Quite frequently, someone will see a picture of a darling little Boston Terrier in a magazine, dog-breed book, or on television, and fall in love with the looks of the dog. Or, having met one of these dogs, a person might be instantly captivated by his charming personality. Then, without a second thought, these people will rush out and buy one, and often they will purchase the first animal they come across.

Unhappily, after living with a dog for a while, some impulsive buyers will come to realize that Bostons have characteristics that they cannot abide. The joyous arrival of a new puppy turns into the daily nightmare of living with a dog that is not suited to the family or individual. This sad situation can be easily avoided by doing a little homework before buying a dog.

There are a number of things you can do to try to determine if a Boston Terrier is the right dog for you. First, read this book. Next, contact the Boston Terrier club nearest you and meet people who own the breed. You can find a club near you by contacting the United Kennel Club or the American Kennel Club (see page 92) and requesting a list of the Boston Terrier clubs in your state.

Once you have contacted people who actually live with a Boston Terrier, you can ask them to tell you about their dog, what it is like living with one, and what they like and do not like about the breed. If possible, you should spend time visiting as many Bostons as you can. If you find one that you especially like, ask who bred the dog and contact that breeder.

There are a number of useful questions you can ask yourself to help you decide if a Boston Terrier is the right breed for you:
✔ What types of inherited or acquired physical problems are known to affect this breed? You must be willing to take care of any such problems that might develop in your dog. Many inherited problems can be treated or corrected, but the cost of the treatment may be more than you are willing or able to afford.

✔ How long can you expect your pet to live? Boston Terriers typically have rather long life spans if well cared for. They can live 12 years or longer.

✔ Does the breed show common temperamental problems? While Boston Terriers are generally sweet dogs, their temperament, which is to say their mental health, will vary from line to line and among individuals. It is important to ensure that you get a dog with a solid, sound temperament.

✔ How do Boston Terriers respond to training? As a rule, they are not the easiest breed to train; however, if you use positive training methods, such as clicker training, they can be taught to obey commands, and even to compete in obedience trials. However, you should

get to know some Bostons to find out if you've got the determination and patience necessary to train one.

✔ Are you (and everyone in your family) willing to care for the dog? Let's be honest about this question. Many people have neither the time nor the desire to give a pet the care it needs. Children, for example, will promise the moon, only to be distracted a week later. Be sure that at least one person (you, for example) will dedicate the necessary time *every* day to adequately care for your dog. Boston Terriers can become unhappy and react negatively, not to mention the possibilities of injury and disease, if they are denied attention and care.

✔ Are you ready to care for a puppy or an older dog? Once again, there must be a solid commitment on the part of at least one person in your family. While puppies are engaging and cute, and for those reasons caring for them might seem relatively easy, you must bear in mind that a growing dog needs to be housetrained and learn all his manners during his first year of life. Training your dog properly will take a large bite out of your time.

Children, Other Pets, and Your Dog

When thinking about a Boston Terrier, you should carefully consider any other pets you may already have in your household. If there is another dog, you must be sure that he will not harm the new one. Because they are small, one bite from a larger dog can seriously injure or even kill a Boston Terrier. Similarly, your Boston Terrier could be injured just by being stepped on by the larger dog. This can also be a danger if you own livestock such as horses.

puppies, are small enough to be seriously hurt by a toddler. Also, the dog might respond by biting the child, or learn to fear all children.

You must also consider elderly members of your family. As people age they may not be able to walk, hear, or see as well as before, and there is a possibility of their stumbling over or stepping on your dog. Very young puppies may not have learned to avoid the feet of family members, and will not realize that they can be hurt.

If you have any doubts about whether a Boston Terrier will work out in your household, consult a competent dog trainer, behaviorist, groomer, veterinarian, or Boston Terrier breeder.

Puppy or Older Dog?

The Puppy

One of the advantages of getting a puppy is that he will grow up with you. This will give you the opportunity to socialize him to your lifestyle, and to teach him as you prefer.

Keep in mind that your Boston Terrier does not think of himself as a small dog, and will not hesitate to confront larger animals.

A small puppy could easily be the victim of an intolerant or jealous cat. One swipe from a cat's claws can permanently injure your Boston Terrier's eyes.

The reactions of children should be a major concern when introducing a new dog into the family. Very young children often cannot understand that the cute little doggie is not just an animated toy. Boston Terriers, especially

A puppy can be a great deal of fun, and his antics can provide you with hours of delight. On the other hand, a puppy will also need more of your time during his first year of life. He will need to be house-trained, obedience-trained, taught not to chew, and so forth. Also, a puppy will require more veterinary care in his first year of life than the yearly maintenance he will need thereafter.

The Older Dog

Because Boston Terriers are not as popular as some other breeds, there are fewer available for adoption. However, sometimes older dogs do come up for adoption or sale. This situation can arise due to the death of the owner, or perhaps the inability of the owner to keep the dog. Sometimes a breeder will offer a retired show dog for adoption or sale. At other times the breeder may determine that a show prospect will not work out, and will put the dog up for adoption or sale.

You should also be aware that people will often put a dog up for adoption because they do not like the way he behaves. This does not necessarily mean that the dog is bad. Behavior that is not acceptable to one person may be perfectly fine, or even desirable, to another.

There are a number of points to consider when acquiring an older dog. You must be aware that the dog will need time to get used to you and your family. The adjustment period can take from three to six months. You cannot "explain" to the dog that your house is now his new home, and he cannot "tell" you about his fears and anxieties.

Sometimes a dog will appear happy and seem to fit in right away, but if you pay close attention you will see him relax and become even more playful and at ease a few months later.

One of the benefits of adopting an older dog is that he will most likely be house-trained and obedience-trained. The dog will be settled and

mature. He will have had all the necessary puppy shots, and will often be neutered or spayed.

If you plan to get a dog as a companion for the elderly, a mature dog may be the best choice, as such a dog will be easier for an older person to handle.

Throughout the country there are groups of people who rescue unwanted dogs of different breeds. These associations are referred to as *breed rescue groups*. A Boston Terrier rescue group is a good place to find an older dog for adoption, since the people who foster the dogs will evaluate them and try to match each dog with the right home.

Male or Female?

Both physically and psychologically, there is not much difference between the male and female Boston Terrier. The female is generally a bit smaller than the male, but not enough to make a big difference.

The temperament in both sexes is about the same. A more important behavioral determinant is the dog's breeding. There is, however, one very important factor over which you have influence, and that is the decision whether or not to spay or neuter your pet.

Unless you are planning to make a commitment to show and breed your dog, both males and females should be "fixed." This operation will eliminate many of the problems associated with each sex. For example, an unneutered male can have accidents or "mark" in your house. This can be either an occasional problem or a regular occurrence. Male dogs can be expected to mark outside, and this can be a problem if you have gardens, unless you train your pet to relieve himself in designated areas only.

If you own an unspayed female, she will come into "season" or "heat" twice a year. During this time you will not be able to trust her outside at all, even on a leash. Male dogs have been known to breed a female while she is on a leash being walked by her owner!

With an intact female you will risk having an unwanted litter of puppies every six months.

Both males and females that are not fixed will have a tendency to roam, the male in pursuit of a female, and the female to let the male know where she lives. Generally, the male will have a greater desire to roam than the female, and will travel a larger area. If given the opportunity, a female in heat will take off in search of a willing male, and you can bet that she will find one.

For small dogs, such as Boston Terriers, there are added dangers inherent in unregulated breeding. If a Boston female breeds with a larger dog, the developing puppies may be too big for her, creating medical problems and possibly even causing the death of the dam. The actual mating itself can cause serious injury to the female if the male is much larger. Therefore, it is especially important to spay those Boston Terrier females that are not slated for a show or breeding program.

There are numerous medical side benefits to fixing your dog. For example, spaying your female before her first heat (between five and six months of age) will greatly reduce the risk of breast cancer. A neutered male will be calmer, making him a nicer family pet. He will be less likely to become aggressive or competitive toward other dogs, and will not chase after a female in heat. Neutering a male will also reduce the risk of certain types of can-

cer. For both sexes, the urge to roam will be reduced and, for both, the life expectancy can also be expected to increase.

What Does Quality Mean?

When you choose a dog, you want to consider the various factors that determine the "quality" of an animal. Some of the myths and misinterpretations concerning the quality of a dog are discussed below.

Papers

It is commonly believed that if a puppy is registered, he is a quality dog. Unfortunately, this is not the case. The American Kennel Club, which is the major registering body for all dogs in this country, is simply a registry service. The registration papers that come with your dog do not guarantee anything except that a history or pedigree of a given dog has been reported to the American Kennel Club, and has been accu-

rately recorded by that agency. Registry is not a guarantee that the puppy you purchase is

✔ healthy,

✔ of sound temperament,

✔ of show quality,

✔ likely to make a good pet,

✔ likely to meet standards for the breed,

✔ free of genetic defects,

✔ or even that the papers that accompany your puppy actually belong to that particular dog.

The validity of the papers issued with your Boston puppy as well as the quality of the puppy you purchase depend entirely upon the ethics of the breeder with whom you deal.

In some cases, a breeder will determine that a puppy has a major flaw that will bar the dog from a show career. Such puppies will be sold as pet quality (usually with a spay/neuter contract). As far as being pets, there is absolutely nothing wrong with such animals, and the overall quality of the dog will be substantially the same as the puppy's show-prospect littermates.

WHERE TO GET A GOOD BOSTON TERRIER

Once you have decided that the Boston Terrier is the right breed for you, you will be faced with the problem of finding an animal of the quality you desire. This will mean locating a good, ethical breeder.

Finding a Breeder

The best place to start the search for an ethical breeder is with your national and/or local Boston Terrier club, or your local Boston Terrier rescue group. You can find out how to contact these organizations through the American Kennel Club.

If a local or national club meets within traveling distance of your home, attend their meetings on a regular basis. Get to know the breeders, and go see their dogs. When you find an animal you like, find out who bred the dog and contact that breeder. If the breeder does not have puppies available but seems to be someone you might trust, see if you can get on a waiting list, or ask to be referred to another breeder.

Because Boston Terriers have small litters and are usually born by C-section, good breeders usually have waiting lists for puppies, and do not need to advertise in newspapers.

Quality Begins with the Breeder

Puppy Mills

Technically speaking, anyone who breeds dogs is considered a "breeder." This includes those people who consider their dogs "cash crops," and simply produce animals without regard for the health and welfare of the dogs. These operations, called "puppy mills," often experience a high rate of disease and mortality among their "products." In some areas of the country the puppy mill may sell directly to the public. Sometimes people find these breeders by taking a drive in the country and seeing a handmade sign in front of a quaint farmhouse offering puppies for sale. The plain clothes of the farmer and his family might make the unsuspecting buyer instantly at ease and foster a feeling of ethics and safety. However, to the puppy-mill "farmer," his puppies are just a cash crop.

Commercial Breeding Operations

Legitimate commercial breeding operations carry certain risks as well. Though the paperwork will usually be in order, the main point of these businesses is to make a profit. The operators might find themselves tempted to cut corners by minimizing medical care, socialization training, and human-animal bonding activities. There will also be more of a chance for a substandard animal to be released from such an operation, as every dog not sold is a financial loss. Puppies produced by puppy mills and commercial breeders are hardly ever of show quality, and many do not even make good pets.

Ethical Breeders

Good breeders and serious hobbyists will want to sell their puppies themselves so they can personally evaluate the prospective buyer. They will offer a health guarantee and will take the puppy back if there is a problem. Ethical breeders put their hearts and souls, as well as a great deal of work, into producing a good line

═══CHECKLIST═══

An Ethical Breeder Will

1 stand behind his or her dogs.
2 answer your questions.
3 breed only one to two litters a year.
4 breed only one or two breeds of dog.
5 have clean facilities.
6 not push breeding contracts.
7 have a good socialization program for the puppies.

of dogs. They will know each animal personally, and will want to place their puppies in a good home.

A good breeder will maintain certain policies as a matter of course. You should ask specifically about the following matters:

Will the breeder stand behind the dog for his entire life? This does not mean that if your dog catches a communicable disease, or is killed in an accident, or dies of old age, that you will get the dog replaced. But it does mean that if your dog develops any inherited or congenital diseases or physical flaws, the breeder will replace the dog or at least work with you to take care of the problem. A good breeder wants to know how his or her dogs develop throughout their lives, as this is the only way to develop good, strong lines.

Will the breeder help you with any questions you may have concerning all aspects of dog ownership? Good breeders want you to be happy with your dog. They do not want you to have to return the dog to them, because this is not in the best interests of the animal. Therefore, they will help you in any way they can, and will try to answer questions you may have about your dog.

Will the breeder tell you about faults of the line and the breeding? There are no perfect dogs. A concerned breeder will tell you as soon as any problem develops in the line, so that you can look for the problem in your pet. You should be warned about any possible defects that might show up in your Boston Terrier.

Will the breeder give as references people who have purchased their dogs? Honest breeders are proud of what they have produced, and will welcome any opportunity to show off. They will be delighted to know that you want

to see their stock and find out how their dogs turn out. It goes without saying that they will want you to talk to satisfied customers.

Does the breeder give the female and puppies the best food, veterinary care, and socialization? A concerned breeder will provide the best care for both the puppies and the dam. This will ensure that you will own a happy, healthy dog.

Will the breeder require you to sign a contract stating that you will adhere to the breeder's or breed club's breeding ethics? Concerned breeders want to ensure that their dogs will be given the best of care, and that you will observe the highest ethical standards with your dog. A contract keeps everything clear, and protects both the seller and buyer.

Remember, geographical location, ethnic background, or religious affiliation of the breeder do not affect the quality of your Boston Terrier. The only guarantee of quality is the personal ethics of your breeder.

How to Select the Right Boston Terrier

A good place to start is to see both the sire (male) and the dam (female) of the litter.

Ask the breeder to give you as much information about the line and the dog as possible. A good breeder will have many stories to tell about the dogs in the pedigree.

Temperament (the dog's mental health) and obedience titles will be more important to you than the number of champions in the pedigree. Championship indicates only that a dog's conformation (how it looks and moves) measures up to the breed standard. It gives no indication of temperament or intelligence, which are the qualities that make a good pet.

If you are a first-time Boston Terrier owner, you may want to let the breeder help you select the right puppy for you. Sometimes a litter of puppies may have an individual that is very dominant or submissive. Extremes in temperament can be difficult to raise if you have not done it before. Because the breeder has studied each puppy from birth, the breeder will be qualified to tell you the temperament of each puppy.

You can also use this general rule of thumb to select a pup: For an average pet, do not take the boldest puppy in the litter, the one that runs to you first and pushes the other puppies out of the way. Such an animal may be difficult to handle. Many people feel that the boldest puppy instantly fell in love with them and fought to be the first to reach them, but this is

not the case. The dog just wanted to maintain his position as a bully, and may try to push you around as well.

You do not want the smallest puppy either. This could be an indication of medical or developmental problems that would not show up until later.

You will not want a puppy that is shy and timid either. Such an animal may have difficulty facing the challenges of life, and may not make a well-adjusted pet.

Choose a puppy that seems interested in you and wants to spend a lot of time with you, the one that is most willing to follow you around. This kind of behavior indicates good balance in mind and body, with a desire to be near humans.

Often a litter consists of only one or two puppies, and they are so close in all aspects that the choice comes down to the one whose looks appeal to you most—and that can be all right, too.

All of the puppies in the litter should be healthy. Their coats should have a healthy shine and they should be neither too fat nor too thin. You should be able to just feel the ribs when you run your fingers over their sides. They should not have fleas and should be clean, with no strong, offensive odor. Watch for disease symptoms such as runny eyes, discharge from the nose, bald patches, sores, and so on.

At What Age to Get a Puppy

Many behaviorists feel that you should get your new puppy at the beginning of the seventh week. However, toy dog expert Darlene Arden states clearly in her book *The Irrepress-*

ible Toy Dog that some puppies need to stay with their mother until twelve weeks of age, so wait until your puppy is twelve weeks old before taking him home. A good breeder will provide the puppy with the important socialization and training needed between seven and twelve weeks.

You should never take a puppy from his mother before seven weeks, since the puppy needs interaction with his mother and littermates until that age. Breeders who are anxious to save money will let puppies go at five and six weeks of age. You do not want to get a puppy from that type of operation.

When to Get a Boston Puppy

Although almost any time can be a good time to get your new puppy, a little planning can be advantageous. If you work and have vacation time, it is best to plan to take off a few days to stay home with your new puppy. This will give your new pet time to bond with you, and he will feel more secure after a few days with you than if he is brought to a new home and left completely alone the very next day. If you cannot take off a day or two, try to bring your puppy home on the evening before you have a few days off, such as a Friday night. This will allow the puppy time to get adjusted. You will be able to take him to the veterinarian for a checkup, and you will be there if the puppy has trouble getting used to different water, food, surroundings, climate, and so on. This last is very important for puppies that are shipped from other parts of the country.

Note: Some people feel that it is easier to house-train a Boston Terrier in the spring because they do not like to take the puppy outside when it is cold.

The arrival of the new puppy should be during a quiet time in your life. Being taken to a new home can be very stressful; you cannot "explain" the new situation to the puppy. Nor can you tell him that you want very much to make the transition as easy and nonthreatening as possible. There are certain times when it is not wise to bring a puppy home, such as holidays, birthdays, or any other time when exciting or traumatic events are taking place. The puppy will be aware of the excitement and tension felt by the family members, and this could add to the stress of being removed from the litter. Your new pet deserves a nice, quiet, loving welcome to his new home.

CARING FOR YOUR BOSTON TERRIER

The advance preparation you make for a new puppy is so important. While you happily anticipate your new Boston's arrival, have everything you will need ready in advance. It's going to be a long, happy relationship, so start it right.

Preparing for the Arrival of Your Boston Puppy

There are some things you will need to do before you bring your new puppy home. A special place must be prepared for your pet and the rest of the house made either off-limits or puppy-proofed. You will need to establish rules and procedures for the care of the puppy, and these rules must be discussed and agreed to by all of the members of your household. Also, there are a number of supplies you will need to have on hand.

A Place of His Own

Dogs are territorial animals, and your puppy will need a place he can think of as his own. You should provide a quiet spot where your puppy can be alone if he wants to. This can be a corner of a room. The spot should contain your pet's sleeping area. You may want to use a child's playpen to keep your new puppy in while you are not at home. This is an ideal, safe way to keep a puppy out of trouble and still allow him enough room to exercise. You can spread newspapers on the bottom of the playpen to take care of accidents.

If you do not plan to keep your puppy in an exercise pen, you should puppy-proof the areas where he will be allowed to go. Puppy-proofing is very similar to child-proofing.

✔ Remove from reach any objects that you do not want chewed. This includes all electrical wires and appliances. It would not hurt to put protective covers on those outlets that are at puppy level.

✔ Check that floor tiles, woodwork, and other surfaces are not painted or treated with toxic materials that would harm your puppy if accidently chewed or licked. It does not take a large quantity of a toxic substance to kill a small Boston Terrier puppy.

✔ All cabinets must be safe from prying puppy paws. This is especially necessary if you plan to confine your pet to the kitchen or bathroom.

✔ Cleansers are a major risk. Be sure to keep a poison hot-line number by your telephone in the event of an accident. You can get these numbers from your veterinarian.

✔ Close off any areas that you do not want the puppy to get into, such as porches, decks, balconies, or fences. You must be concerned about your pet slipping through fences, gates, or iron grillwork. If you have a fenced-in yard, be sure that there are no little holes for the puppy to squeeze through. Even if there is only one small hole in your fence, your puppy will find it!

✔ Be careful around stairs; a clumsy little puppy can easily slip on them and could be seriously hurt or even killed. The most dangerous steps are the type that have open risers.

Review all of the dangers in your house with all of the members of your family. Everyone must learn to watch out for the puppy, so as not to step on him or catch him in a closing door. Because Boston Terriers are very intelligent dogs, it should not take long before the puppy learns to avoid some of the dangers of your home. But until that time you must watch out for him.

Supplies

Food: It is a good idea to find out which food the breeder uses and buy that brand. Using the same brand will provide some continuity in your pet's life, so that he will have something familiar in the midst of all the new experiences. If the brand of food that the breeder uses is an inexpensive supermarket brand, you should not keep your puppy on that brand of food. Be sure to use a premium, all-natural brand. Switching your puppy from one food to another takes about a week (see page 46, Changing Brands of Food).

Bowls: Make sure that food and water bowls are as tip-proof as possible. It is better to have two separate bowls rather than two bowls in one container. If the bowls are attached you will have to disturb both water and food each time you want to change one.

Crate: You should provide a special sleeping area for your pet. This can be a basket with a dog bed in it, but a canine carrying crate has a number of advantages that should be considered. It will provide the puppy with a secure feeling. While it is not a good idea to keep a dog crated all day long, having him sleep in a crate will help him get used to being in one in the event that you need to transport your pet. The best style of crate that allows the maximum amount of air circulation is the open wire-type crate.

You can purchase a crate cover for an open wire crate for use in cooler temperatures or when you want to keep your pet warm. The crate should be large enough to hold a full-

═CHECKLIST═

Supplies
1 Food
2 Bowls
3 Crate
4 Dog bed
5 Collar and leash
6 Brush and comb
7 Nail clippers
8 Styptic powder
9 Toys

grown Boston Terrier with a few inches to spare. An adult dog should be able to stand up and turn around. You will need to supply soft bedding that can be easily changed or cleaned.

Dog bed: Be selective when choosing a dog bed. Ideally the dog bed should provide cushioning for your dog. Boston Terriers do not have natural padding in the form of a dense coat or a layer of fat; therefore, lying on hard surfaces can be uncomfortable. The dog bed should not be stuffed with anything that can

dry out, such as foam rubber or cedar shavings. The ideal bedding is made of imitation lamb's wool or filled with the type of batting used to make quilts.

Toys: You must provide your pet with some toys to chew on. The puppy should not have rawhide, real bones, toys made of fabric, or soft plastic toys that can be chewed into little pieces and swallowed. It is not a good idea to give him old shoes, slippers, or any other type of clothing. Puppies cannot tell the difference between old shoes and new, and may chew up the new pair of shoes you were going to wear to the party tomorrow night.

Collar and leash: You will need a collar and leash. Make sure the leash is strong without being too heavy. Never put a choke-type collar on a puppy. A martingale nylon collar works best.

TIP

Toys

✔ They should be hard nylon or rubber.
✔ They should not be anything that can be chewed or swallowed, string, edible products, or parts of animals.

Brush and comb: Be sure to obtain the proper kind of brush for your dog. Because their coat is short, Boston Terriers need a soft bristle brush. Wire brushes can hurt their skin. A special flea comb is also necessary to check your dog for fleas.

Nail clippers: You will also want to have nail clippers on hand, as well as some styptic powder to stop the bleeding if you should happen to clip the nails too short. (Do your best to avoid the pink "quick," but mishaps may occur from time to time.) Styptic powder or sticks for dogs can be purchased at any pet-supply store.

Bringing Your New Puppy Home

When the day finally comes to take your darling little puppy home you will be very excited, but you should attempt to remain calm. If you are going to drive to pick up your pet, it will be best to transport him home in his new crate. As tempting as it may be to let the puppy sit on your lap, this is not a safe way to travel. It is best to keep the new puppy in his new crate, which you have lined with newspapers and an old towel. This way, you will keep him from wiggling off your lap and onto the floor, where he could easily crawl under a seat and get into trouble. If the puppy has a nature call or gets sick in your lap or on the floor of the car, it can be very distracting.

Be sure to bring along plenty of paper towels and water in a container just in case. If children are along for the ride, do not allow them to poke at the puppy, play with him, or jostle his crate. Try to make the ride as quiet as possible to reduce stress. If you want to play music on the radio, select something peaceful and soothing.

inside, take him to the special place you have prepared, and let him explore and settle down. If your trip lasted more than four hours you can give the puppy a small amount of food and water right away; otherwise, it is best to wait a little while for things to calm down.

After about an hour, you can give the puppy something to eat (if it is his normal feeding time) and drink. After eating and drinking the puppy may want to sleep. If this is the case, take him out as soon as he wakes up.

Generally, you should let the puppy decide what he wants to do rather than forcing him to do what you want. Play with him only if he wants to. Let him sleep when he is tired. Try to give him at least a day to settle in before allowing friends to come and meet your delightful new friend. It would also help to keep the household quiet for at least the first day until the puppy has had a chance to explore and feel secure about his new home.

How to Carry Your New Puppy

You should never hold a puppy under his front legs with the hind legs hanging down for an extended period of time. Nor should you pick up your puppy by the scruff of the neck as the mother dog does.

It is very important to teach children how to hold a puppy properly since they have a tendency to hold them under their front legs and swing them around. Puppies should be carried in such a way that the entire body is supported. Always maintain a firm grip on the puppy so that he cannot wriggle out of your hands and fall. For a small Boston puppy, a fall from three to four feet up can cause serious injury.

If the trip is going to be long, stop often to allow the puppy to exercise and take nature breaks. Always keep your new pet on a leash when you do this so that he cannot run away or get hurt. Do not feed the puppy during the trip unless you plan to be driving more than six hours. You can give him a few laps of water, but do not let him drink too much or he may get sick. If the puppy sleeps during the trip, be sure to take him out as soon as possible after he wakes up, as he will surely need a nature break.

When You First Arrive Home

When you arrive home, give the puppy a chance to walk outside and take a break before going inside. As soon as you bring your pet

The best way to safely carry a puppy is to hold him with one hand supporting his front legs and the other hand supporting his back legs.

Socialization

After your pup has adjusted to his new home and has been to the veterinarian for a checkup and shots, you can start a socialization program.

Socializing a puppy is one of the most important things you can do to ensure that he grows up to be a happy, well-adjusted dog. An unsocialized puppy can grow up to become so fearful and destructive that you may not be able to keep him. A well-socialized puppy is a happy puppy, and will grow up to be a happy adult dog that will be able to take things as they come.

Puppies do not have the life experience needed to handle many of the strange sounds, sights, and smells that they will encounter. It is easy to forget that the new puppy has been alive for only two to three months, and that he was isolated with his mother for most of that time. Also, keep in mind that in one year your puppy is going through all of the mental and physical growth stages that humans take decades to accomplish. You do not have years to accomplish a meaningful socialization process, but months at best.

Handling

An important part of the socialization program must include handling your puppy. If your breeder has done a good job, you can continue the training where it was left off. You must touch all parts of your dog's body. This will get your dog used to being handled, and in time he will come to enjoy the contact.

It will also make it much easier if you or your veterinarian need to give medical attention to your pet. Grooming will be easier as well.

You will want to handle the dog's face, ears, mouth, belly, feet, tail, toes, toenails, and the pads of his feet. Be sure to reward your pet for letting you do these things to him. Get your puppy used to being rolled over onto his back, held down on his side, and being held in your arms.

Going Outside

The next part of socialization occurs outside the house. Begin by taking your new puppy to many different places, such as the park, for a walk down the street, to a playground, to watch children play, to puppy kindergarten

classes, to friends' houses, and so on. In other words, any place that is safe, yet active.

You do not want to subject your puppy to loud noise at close range or to other situations that may frighten him. Use your judgment as to what is safe. Also, bear in mind that some puppies seem to go through a "fright" stage at around eight weeks of age. If you notice that your pet seems unusually unsure or cautious, try to be more cautious until this phase has passed.

Overprotecting Your Puppy

Because Boston Terrier puppies are so cute and small, you may experience a tendency to want to carry your pet around. This is not a good practice, because the puppy may become dependent upon you and become frightened when you put him down. It is important to avoid cuddling the puppy too much, or becoming overprotective. This, too, could develop into overdependency. If this happens you will find it difficult to leave your pet alone without him suffering anxiety.

If the puppy develops into an anxious dog, he may become destructive, or a nonstop barker. It is best to try to solve these problems when the dog is young. In some cases, allowing your dog to sleep in bed with you or go on the furniture is often the root cause of behavior problems that develop later in the dog's life. As tempting as it may be, do not allow your dog to sleep in bed with any member of the family or go on the furniture.

A well-socialized puppy will make a good companion that will enjoy going places with you and having fun, and that will be capable of being left alone when necessary without becoming sad.

Starting Obedience Training

As soon as the puppy is old enough, you should start obedience training. Most trainers will not start a dog on obedience training until he is six months of age. If you cannot find a trainer who will start your dog at a younger age, enroll the dog in a puppy kindergarten class. Using gentle and informal methods, puppies can be taught obedience from eight weeks of age.

Some people feel that their dogs listen to them well enough without training, but even a well-behaved dog should receive obedience training. A well-behaved dog is always a welcome guest. An obedience-training class is also part of your dog's socialization (see page 81 for a discussion of obedience training).

As your Boston Terrier gets older, you should continue to take him to as many places as possible so that your pet does not become a "house potato."

Introducing New Babies and Pets

From time to time a new member is added to the family. This could be a baby, an older person, a cat, a dog, or some other pet. And sometimes your Boston Terrier may not welcome this addition. This could be especially true if the new arrival is a mature dog.

If an adult dog is coming into the household, the best way to handle the situation is to make arrangements for the two dogs to meet on neutral ground, then neither dog will feel as though the other is an intruder into his territory, and they will be more likely to become friends. After a few visits on neutral ground, you can walk both dogs to your home. This way you avoid putting either dog in the

situation where one is an intruder and one a defender of the home.

If the new addition is a baby, you must pay close attention to the amount and quality of time you spend with your dog before the baby's arrival. Afterwards, try to keep the amount and quality of time with the dog unchanged. Do not get angry at the dog for his curiosity toward the baby. Nor should you correct your pet in such a way that the dog could associate the correction with the baby. You should make contact with the baby a happy playtime for the dog, even though you are the one who will be playing with the dog and not the baby. The dog will then associate the baby with the fun times he has with you.

Contact between baby and dog is a very personal matter. You will have to set the limits.

Always consult your pediatrician about this, and do what you feel is best. If at any time you do not feel comfortable allowing your dog to be around the baby, do not permit it.

When a baby starts to crawl or walk, your dog may react with renewed interest. Always try to make the encounter a happy time for the dog by playing with him. Never scold the dog for going near the baby and never leave the baby and dog together unsupervised.

As soon as your baby starts to move around you should teach the child how to behave toward animals. Never leave an unsupervised toddler around your dog. No matter how friendly they are toward each other, a Boston Terrier can be hurt by a falling child. The child will want to pull ears, poke eyes, and otherwise explore the dog as if he were a toy. This should not be allowed.

With a little planning and thought, children and dogs can get along just fine. They can grow together, forming a special bond that adults often seem to miss.

Boarding Your Boston Terrier

To find a good boarding facility, consult a number of professionals, such as your veterinarian, dog groomer, pet-supply store, and dog trainer. Once you have a number of possible kennels to choose from, go and see the facilities.

The boarded dogs should look reasonably happy and clean. There should not be a strong, offensive odor. The dogs should have adequate space to exercise, and there should be an outside play area for them. Cats, dogs, and birds should not be kept in the same room. The kennel should have a flea-control program, and you should ask the manager to explain it to you in detail.

With a little bit of research, you should be able to find a place where you can leave your dog without worry or concern. Most dogs find the activities at a boarding kennel interesting, and do not pine for their owners. In many cases, dogs that are left at a boarding facility do fine.

Be sure to let your veterinarian know that your dog is being boarded, and leave instructions on how you want your dog cared for in the event of an emergency.

You can bring along your dog's favorite toy or blanket if you wish, but often these items will get lost in the shuffle of the day-to-day kennel operation, so do not send along your best toys or blankets. An old towel will give your dog something that has your scent on it to snuggle into. You should also bring along your dog's food. Boarding kennels vary as to what they feed their boarders; often they will use one brand of food for all of the dogs. Even if this is a premium-quality food, it may upset your dog's digestion just because it is different, and cause your dog to develop diarrhea. Also remember to bring any medication your dog needs while you are away, with detailed written instructions for use. If your dog is due to get heartworm medication, be sure to include it.

Pet-sitters

There are some alternatives to boarding your pet if you must leave him at home when you travel. One possibility is to have a pet-sitter take care of your dog. Pet-sitters are people who will come to your home a number of times a day to walk, feed, and play with your dog while you are away. You should always interview a pet-sitter and ask for references. Once you select someone, ask him or her to come over while you are home to learn the routines and know where everything is kept. This will also allow the dog and the pet-sitter to get to know each other. Sometimes a neighbor can watch your dog while you are gone and act as a pet-sitter. Sometimes a pet-sitter may stay in your home and be a house-sitter as well. This will help to ensure that your home and dog are safe while you are away. Always be sure to leave detailed instructions for the sitter, explaining what needs to be done. Go over these instructions with the sitter to make sure that they are understood.

Friends or Relatives

Another alternative to a boarding kennel is to allow your dog to stay with friends or relatives. Again, a preintroduction to the friend or relative would make the stay for your dog much less stressful, and detailed, written instructions should be left for the dog.

Traveling by Car with Your Boston Terrier

Advance planning makes traveling with your dog a pleasure for you both. Always use a crate or special harness. This keeps your dog safe from accident or theft and your car safe from damage by the dog.

Never leave your dog alone in a closed car. Summer temperatures can make a closed car a deathtrap in minutes—especially for the short-faced, dark-coated Boston. If you must leave your dog in the car, open the windows slightly and keep the stop short!

Drive with the air conditioning on in warm weather. Otherwise open the windows slightly for air circulation, but not enough for the dog to put his head out. Many dogs love doing this, but it is very dangerous for them and for human passengers as well.

Have an ample supply of bottled drinking water handy and enough cool tap water to douse a dog suffering from the heat. In cold weather, most Bostons will appreciate a warm coat or sweater.

Schedule rest stops every few hours and walk your dog on leash. Be sure the dog has an I.D. tag and permanent identification such as a microchip. Carry a recent photo of your pet in case he goes missing.

If your dog suffers from motion sickness, withhold food and water for several hours before a trip. Dogs usually overcome this problem in time if they are taken for short trips to "fun" places such as parks, dog runs, or homes of friends. Dogs that are driven only to the veterinarian's office soon learn to dislike car travel. If necessary, pills are available to help with this problem. Consult your veterinarian for the right medication to give your dog. Motion sickness is usually a problem of conditioning, so slowly increase trips to make them fun. Your dog should become an avid traveler in no time.

HOW-TO: HOUSE-TRAIN

✔ You have two choices for housetraining: outside, or in a doggie litter box. The doggie litter box is convenient for people with mobility problems or who live in apartments or where winters are severe.

✔ Choose the exact spot for the toilet area, either the litter box or the outdoor toilet spot. It should always be the same location. The outside area must be well marked so that your dog can identify it as the toilet area.

✔ Each time that your dog needs to relieve himself, take him to the toilet area. Do not play with your dog on the way to this area. If you have a very young puppy carry him to this area. Praise your dog when he eliminates, giving him a treat. Say something like "*Good potty.*"

✔ As your dog learns to relieve himself in the designated area, add a signal word to the process that lets the dog know that you want him to use the toilet area. Some people say "*Do your business*" or "*Do you have to go potty?*"

Accidents

If your dog has an accident outside of the designated area, do not get upset, stick his nose in it, and spank him. Do not let the dog see you cleaning the area or call attention to it in any way. If you do, you will teach your dog to relieve himself outside the designated area and you will increase the dog's stress level, making it more difficult for your dog to control himself.

Diet

Diet is very important in house-training. Higher quality food decreases the dog's need to eliminate.

House-training Specifics

Young puppies require more patience if house-training is to be successful.

Your puppy will need time to develop physically before he can control his bodily functions. At key times your puppy will need to relieve himself:

✔ After waking up
✔ After playing
✔ After eating
✔ And if sniffing around, looking for a spot.

Keep these key times in mind and apply them to your house-training plan. Take your puppy outside or to a litter box immediately at any of these times. This means that you must monitor your puppy so that you know the instant he needs to go out. You will make some mistakes from time to time, but as you learn to read your puppy's

body language you will get better at knowing when he needs to relieve himself. Do not get upset if you miss a few times and your puppy has an accident in the house or outside of his litter box. This will not undo the training and successes that you have made together up to now.

When you see that it is time for a "potty run," pick up your puppy and take him to the designated area. By doing this, you will help the puppy to hold it until you put him down again. When you reach the designated area, put your puppy on the ground and leave him alone. Your puppy will need a few minutes to get his bearings and realize that you have taken him to the potty area. If your puppy relieves himself, immediately praise him lavishly and give him a special food treat. If you think that your puppy is not finished, leave him alone so he has time to finish doing what he must. If your puppy does not relieve himself within the next five minutes, bring him back inside or take him out of the litter box and try again in ten minutes. However, during that ten minutes never take your eyes off your puppy.

If you carefully keep track of the number of times and about when your puppy moves his bowels and urinates in the course of a day, you will soon get to know your puppy's routine. This will give you a good idea when a potty break is necessary and when your puppy is finished. Puppies usually need to move their bowels after every meal. However, they will normally need to urinate more often.

Once your puppy is finished, you can play a game together or enjoy a brisk walk to somewhere fun. If your puppy learns that part of his reward after relieving himself is a play session and some walk time, your puppy will hurry to relieve himself so that he can have some fun with you. This will prove very handy when the time you have to walk your puppy is limited because of a tight schedule. Not playing with or walking your puppy each time will only enhance the puppy's effort to please you. It will not undo any of your earlier training.

If your puppy does have an accident, simply clean the accident with a solution of white vinegar and water. Fill an 8-ounce measuring cup 3/4 full with water and fill the rest with the vinegar; you will have the correct solution. If the puppy urinated on your carpet, soak up as much liquid as you can with paper towels. Then wet the area with the vinegar solution as deep as the urine went into the carpet. Next use more paper towels to soak up as much of the liquid as possible. If you wish, you can then heap baking soda on the area, which will draw the rest of the moisture out of the carpet. When the baking soda no longer turns yellow, let it set for a few hours and then clean it up. After vacuuming a few times, the powdery residue will come up. Be sure to test a small area first before you try this on your carpet.

Again, never let your puppy see you cleaning up the mess and never, never scold your puppy if he has an accident.

If your puppy came from an ethical breeder, he will have a natural desire to keep his personal area clean. It is for this reason that you should not crate a puppy as part of his housetraining. If a young puppy is not physically able to "hold it," you will force the puppy to lie near his accident. By keeping a puppy in a playpen, exercise pen, or a large area, the puppy can move away from his sleeping area to relieve himself. Puppies that were born and raised in puppy mills or sold through pet shops have often been born and raised in a dirty environment and will not have the natural desire to stay clean. These puppies may take longer to house-train.

FEEDING YOUR BOSTON TERRIER

We have all heard the expression "You are what you eat." Although usually applied to humans, this nutritional cliché is equally true for dogs. If you want your puppy to grow up to be the best possible dog, you must feed him the best possible food. Young dogs often look healthy no matter what they eat, but as they get older they will show the effects of a poor diet.

Diet Is Important

Nutritious food gives your Boston Terrier the ability to withstand illness, the stress of routine health care (such as dental work, spaying, or neutering), and the minor scrapes and bruises that are an inevitable result of an active dog's life. A good diet will help your dog to live longer and to remain healthier.

What is a good diet? It is one that is nutritionally complete and includes plenty of fresh, clean water. Water is often an overlooked part of a dog's diet. It must be fresh, which means you must change it a few times a day. This is very important all year-round. People often forget to keep their dog's water fresh in winter because the dog does not seem to drink as much.

Types of Dog Food

Many new types and varieties of dog food come on the market each year. As they do, it becomes increasingly difficult to determine which food is best for your dog. Because many manufacturers claim that their product is the best value, and all claim to meet canine needs, it will be up to you to determine which food is really best for your pet.

Dog food falls into three basic categories:
✔ dry
✔ wet
✔ semimoist

Protein and fat content are generally offered in the following combinations:
✔ high protein–high fat
✔ medium protein–medium fat

✔ high protein–medium fat

✔ low protein–low fat

The quality of the ingredients generally ranges from "super premium" through "premium," "performance," "regular," to "economy."

Although virtually all commercial dog foods will provide adequate nutrition for your dog, some will be superior and others may not work as well. The prime determinant will be your dog. You will want to choose a food that keeps your pet active and good-looking, one that will not cause him to become either overweight or underweight.

Food Brands

It is a good idea to start with a brand of food that is made from ingredients meant for human consumption and, if possible, organic. These foods typically offer the highest quality available in a pet food. Many dog experts agree that raw fruits and vegetables are an excellent addition to your dog's food since they provide the enzymes and amino acids that help keep your dog healthy. As a general rule of thumb, brands that are sold in supermarkets or discount stores are the lowest quality food, even if the brand is well known. Just like some human products, brands may have an economy blend for discount stores and a premium blend for pet stores.

Properties of Various Foods

Different types of food contain different amounts of moisture. Canned food has the most water added to the food, so in essence you are paying for water. Dry food has the least amount of water, and semimoist is in between.

While the cost of the food is not always an indication of quality, better-quality foods usu-ally end up costing less per serving, because the dog does not need to eat as much. Some dog foods are priced in the super-premium range, but their ingredients actually place them in the premium level, so read the labels carefully.

One of the nicer aspects of feeding your dog an easily digestible food is that the dog will need to eat less and will therefore have less to eliminate. Some foods are loaded with red dye, sugar, or fiber and actually act as diuretics and laxatives, which can cause young dogs to have house-training difficulties.

At various times throughout your dog's life you will need to reevaluate the diet to determine whether it is providing the proper balance of nutrients. As your dog becomes older, his dietary needs will change. Fortunately, if you choose a premium-quality food, the manufacturer will usually offer a variety of formulas for dogs of different ages.

You can use puppy food for your Boston Terrier until he reaches maturity, at which point you can start using a maintenance-level food designed for young to middle-aged adults. As your pet gets older you can either continue with the adult food or, if you and your veterinarian think it's appropriate, you can switch to a light formula. This will ensure that your pet gets the best possible food throughout his life.

Another possibility is to cook your own dog food. As people become more health conscious, opting to make their own meals from "scratch" rather than purchasing prepared foods, they sometimes decide to extend the practice to their pets. However, experts generally advise against this, as it can be difficult to maintain the correct balance of essential ingredients needed to keep your dog healthy. Also, as your dog's needs change, you must reevaluate the contents of your homemade food.

Selecting a Dog Food

There are a number of reasons why you should consider buying only a premium food for your Boston Terrier. An important characteristic of such a product is that the contents will remain consistent from batch to batch. Producers of lower-quality dog foods cannot guarantee that the food you purchase will have the same ingredients four months from now as it has today. This is because the producers purchase ingredients in bulk, buying whatever is a good deal at the time. Because availability depends upon such factors as weather, what is harvested at a given time of year, market conditions, and so on, they never know what will be on the market. Therefore, one item may be the primary ingredient for one batch and a different one for another. Premium dog foods are prepared according to an invariable formula, so they will always taste and look the same.

Premium dog food should not include soybean meal, soy flour, or corn-gluten meal as its main or secondary source of protein. Nor should dog food contain a great deal of meat-and-bone meal. A better ingredient would be beef, lamb, fish, or poultry.

For more information about dog food, go to your local library and read a copy of the Association of American Feed Control Officials' (AAFCO's) complete listing of ingredients and their definitions, as well as pet-food regulations.

Remember, it is up to you to determine the quality of the food you feed your dog.

Snacks

Many people like to give their dogs snacks or treats. There are many such items on the market. Generally, for a small dog such as the Boston Terrier, you should be very careful *not* to allow your dog to have many snacks. If everyone in a large household gave their dog one or two snacks each day, the total could add up to more than the entire day's ration of food. Many breeders and pet owners will not allow snacks at all. Some permit treats only as a reward during training.

Table scraps generally fall into the snack category because they are not the main source of the dog's food. Some people will not allow table scraps or any type of "people food" at all.

Others will permit table scraps only in moderation. If your dog is very active, a small treat once a day or so will do no harm. However, as your Boston Terrier gets older, he may not be able to burn up extra calories added to the diet in the form of snacks.

If you decide to feed your pet commercially prepared dog treats, study the labels as carefully as you would for the primary food. It is unwise to be selective about your dog's main food and then feed him lesser-quality snacks.

Changing Brands of Food

Sometimes it is necessary to change from one brand of food to another. Your veterinarian may recommend this because your dog has developed an allergy to a certain type of food, or the nutritional needs of your pet may change as he gets older.

Generally, it is not a good idea to change foods often. Before you do so, give the matter some serious thought, and always discuss it with your veterinarian. If you find that you must change dog food, introduce the new brand gradually into your pet's diet. A sudden change of food may result in digestive upsets, including diarrhea. Start by adding 20 percent of the new food to 80 percent of the old. In succeeding days increase the percentage of new food. You should allow a week or more for the changeover.

Feeding Schedules

Dogs often do not like their daily schedules changed, and this includes feeding time. Your dog will be happier if you feed him at about the same time every day. However, under special circumstances, if you cannot feed your dog at his normal time, do not despair; dogs are very resilient and can handle an occasional change.

Frequency

Establishing a feeding schedule also means deciding how many meals you will give your dog each day. Opinions vary widely on this point and depend on a variety of factors. Generally, one plan that works is as good as any other plan that works. At one time it was believed that one meal a day was sufficient to meet the needs of a healthy adult dog. But growing numbers of dog owners are moving away from this approach and adopting other sensible feeding regimens.

Feeding Puppies

Most young puppies going into new homes will be on four meals a day, with the number decreasing as the puppy grows. Whenever a new puppy is acquired, the breeder should

➤BOSTON PERSONALS◄

Sam Anderson says, "Ringo watched me make Caesar salads; he figured that he had to tear up the lettuce as I do before he could eat it. Ringo loves carrots. I brought home a 20-pound bag of carrots and before I knew it the bag was getting empty. I found carrots stuck in my shoes in the closet! He also sits for hours on a stool in the kitchen and watches squirrels. Now he is a good birder too. Ringo loves his Sunday frozen yogurt cone. I stopped to buy some fruit and Ringo took the cone from the front seat holder to the back seat without spilling a drop on his way. He was holding it with his paws eating his cone when I returned to the car. To this day I don't know how he did it."

always include a diet sheet and feeding schedule with the essential documents. Most will also include a small quantity of the food the puppy has been getting to avoid the upsets mentioned earlier in this chapter.

Ask your veterinarian and the breeder for advice on when to make changes in the feeding schedule of a growing puppy. If your feeding plan does not seem to work well, you may need to try another approach.

Feeding the Adult Boston

A healthy adult dog can get along well on one meal, although most owners who use this plan will offer a snack of some sort during the day to tide the dog over. Many dog owners feel that dividing the same amount of food into two equal meals keeps a dog more satisfied in the course of a normal day.

Keep in mind that dogs fed a single meal early in the day will be able to move their bowels well before bedtime and so sleep more comfortably than dogs fed one meal in the late afternoon or early evening.

Never allow your dog to be disturbed during meals. If there are other pets or children in the household, feed the dog in his crate.

Feeding Utensils

In addition to using tip-proof bowls (see page 30, Supplies) make sure that the bowls are easy to clean. They should be washed in hot, soapy water after each use and allowed to dry.

As important as food bowls is the container in which the food supply is stored. Dry food should be kept in a covered container that will discourage light, dust, and any pests looking for a free meal. The container should be stored in a cool, dry place that is convenient for the owner to use.

Water

Always provide clean, fresh water for your Boston. Important every day of the year, water is even more vital in warm weather. The short-nosed Boston Terrier can get into serious trouble if there is no access to water on a hot, summer day.

A Final Thought

The quality of a dog's diet shows in his vitality and condition. If a dog is brimming with energy and shows good muscle tone, correct weight and a thick, shiny coat, he is surely being fed properly.

GROOMING YOUR BOSTON TERRIER

Grooming the Boston Terrier is a rather easy task; fancy tools and techniques are not required. Most Boston Terrier's love to be rubbed with a soft towel and brushed with a soft natural bristle brush.

Grooming your Boston Terrier will mean only regular brushing and an occasional bath. Since the Boston's coat is so short, you can wipe the dog down with a damp towel should he get soiled while playing outside. The show dog will need a little more care, but nothing elaborate is required.

It is a good idea to have a full grooming session with your dog at least once a week, in the course of which you should brush his coat, and check his ears, nails, teeth, and eyes. By giving your pet a weekly going-over, you will be more likely to spot any developing problems such as lumps, bumps, and scrapes. You will also find any ticks or fleas that may have been picked up.

The Coat

A Boston Terrier's coat is smooth, bright, and fine in texture. A healthy diet and a little care on your part will keep it that way.

The main grooming tool for the coat is a brush. It should have medium to soft bristles, so that you do not hurt the dog. Natural bristles will work best with the Boston Terrier.

It is important to introduce your dog to the grooming routine early in life. Generally, you should start about a week after you bring your pet home.

✔ Put him on a table or other raised place, such as a bench, countertop, or grooming table. Always have a hand on the dog so that he cannot jump from the table and injure himself.

✔ Run the brush over the dog's body, petting and talking to him all the while. Stroke with the hair, not against it. Be careful not to push the brush down too hard or you could hurt your dog. Do not neglect the ears, feet, toes, and tail area.

✔ You should brush the dog at least every other day, and each grooming session should not take more than 15 minutes.

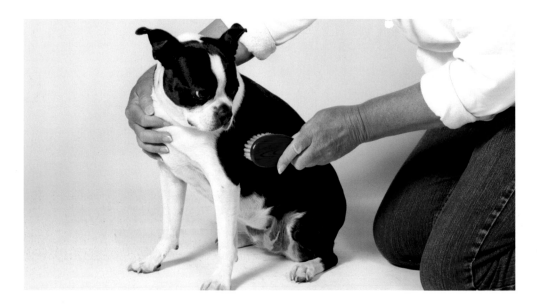

If your dog does not like to be handled, give him a treat each time you touch sensitive areas. Gradually, make the dog let you handle more body areas to earn the treat. Eventually, your pet should relax.

The Nails

Your Boston Terrier's nails should be kept very trim and not be so long as to catch your eye when you look at the feet. If you keep the nails trimmed, the *quick* (the part that bleeds) will stay back at the nail base and not grow forward. If you neglect the nails, the quick will grow, and you will have to trim the nails diligently to get the quick to recede again.

There are three styles of nail clippers on the market. One is a guillotine type, which has two opposed blades between which you insert the nail. Then, a squeeze of a lever chops off the tip of the nail. The second type is scissors with

rounded blades. The third type is a grinding tool. All types work well, so the choice is purely a matter of personal preference.

You should keep *styptic powder* handy to stop bleeding when it occurs. This powder can be purchased at any pet-supply store. Another useful tool is a nail file, which can be used to smooth sharp edges after clipping the nails.

The Ears

By checking your dog's ears on a regular basis you will catch any problems while they are still developing. Look for excessive wax, inflammation, or a strong, foul odor. Frequent head-shaking or a show of pain when the dog's ears are touched or scratched warrants an immediate trip to the veterinarian.

You should check your pet's ears at least once a week. It you notice a wax buildup, you can clean them out with a special preparation, which you can purchase from your veterinarian or pet-supply store. Alternatively, your veterinarian may tell you how to clean your pet's ears using household products.

Never put anything in your dog's ears without first checking with your veterinarian.

The Teeth

It is important to brush your dog's teeth on a regular basis. If you start when your pet is a puppy, he will learn to enjoy the attention. You must use a baby toothbrush, or one that was designed for canine use. Use a special canine toothpaste, which is available from your veterinarian or local pet-supply store. You should *never* use human toothpaste for a dog, as it could be toxic to your pet.

When brushing your dog's teeth, be sure to clean all surfaces—top, bottom, inside, outside, front, and back. Brush the teeth in the same

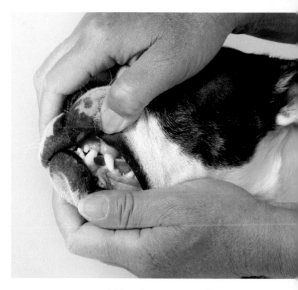

pattern as you would brush your own. Always brush from gum to tooth tip, so you do not push any tartar under the gums.

If your dog will allow you to do so, you can floss his teeth as well.

Some dogs will not permit their teeth to be brushed. There are also finger toothbrushes that work well. You can rub the teeth with baking soda or canine toothpaste, and a soft cloth. This will help to keep your dog's breath smelling sweet.

You should take your dog to the veterinarian every six months for a checkup. At that time your veterinarian will see if the dog's teeth need to be cleaned. If you notice bad breath not caused by eating something that has a foul odor, you should take him in for a checkup. Persistent bad breath in dogs usually indicates oral disease.

Dogs, just like people, are subject to gum diseases and infections. If left untreated, these can lead to serious complications.

The Eyes

Your dog's eyes should not require special care. However, if you go walking in an area of high weeds or brush, you should check your pet's eyes afterward to see if any seeds or pollen are causing irritation. The dog will show signs of irritation by pawing at the eyes, excessive watering, or persistent blinking.

If you suspect that there is something in the dog's eyes, rinse them with warm water. *Do not try to pull back the eyelids to check the eyes.* If the problem does not resolve within an hour or so you should call your veterinarian. Yellow or green mucus discharge from the eyes is a sign of possible infection; you should consult your veterinarian without delay.

Odor

Although Boston Terriers do not usually have a strong odor, you will sometimes notice a foul or musky scent about your dog. Generally, a bath will not solve this problem. The odor is caused by secretions from the *anal sacs,* located beneath the anal sphincter muscle and emptying into the anus via small tubes.

Some of the odorous fluid can be expressed by periodically depressing the anal sacs. Your veterinarian can do this for you, and a good groomer will do it as part of a routine grooming session (be sure to ask). Or you can learn to do the job yourself. Dogs that are more active are less likely to require expression of their sacs; older and less active dogs may need to be checked more often. Generally, you should not need to do this with a puppy. However, if you see your dog scooting his rump along the ground or chewing or licking his rectal area, it usually means that the anal sacs need to be expressed. This is the dog's way of trying to do this on his own.

When and if the anal sacs become blocked, which happens occasionally, have them cleaned out by your veterinarian.

HOW–TO: BATHE YOUR

Because the Boston Terrier is an easy dog to keep clean, it should not be necessary to bathe your dog often—perhaps about twice a year, in the spring and fall. This helps the dog shed his summer and winter coat. It is amazing how your dog will love to wallow in muddy water, yet hate a nice clean bath! By being gentle with your dog while handling him before, during, and after the bath, you will help him enjoy the bath. It is important that you do not allow your dog to drink soapy bathwater or eat any soap. Remember, it does not take a large quantity of soap to make a small dog sick. During the bathtime, take extra precaution that your dog does not jump out of the tub. He could be seriously injured. If necessary, have someone help you restrain the dog.

Note: The bathtime is an excellent opportunity to do your weekly check of your dog's ears, eyes, nails, and overall condition.

Where to Bathe the Dog

You can bathe a Boston Terrier anywhere the dog will fit and that is safe—the kitchen sink, a laundry tub, or a bathtub. It is not a good idea to bathe your dog outside using a garden hose. First, you need warm water, and second, if your dog decides he does not like this method, he may slip away from you and run away.

If you bathe your dog in a bathtub or other deep vessel, stand the dog on a raised, stable platform so he is not at the bottom of the tub. This will reassure a dog that might be afraid of standing in a deep tub. Also be sure to use a bath or sink mat, or other non-skid pad for safe footing. If your dog should slip, he could become frightened or even injured.

Preparation

You will need to gather all of your supplies before you start, but never leave your dog alone in a bath while you look for something that you forgot. You should have the following:

✔ Dog shampoo. Do not use cleansers or laundry detergent; they can hurt your dog, especially if they get in the dog's eyes, mouth, and ears. Read the instructions on the shampoo bottle so that you know ahead of time how to use the product.

✔ A creme rinse. If you decide that you want to use one, you can find good brands for dogs. Be sure to read the directions before you start the bath.

✔ A hose sprayer and containers for water such as a plastic cup (nothing that can break if you drop it).

✔ A soft facecloth and a small sponge.

✔ Rubber gloves and tissues or cotton balls if you plan to express the anal sacs at this time.

✔ Enough dry, soft towels to dry your dog after the bath. I do not recommend using an electric hair dryer, as the short coat on a Boston makes it very easy to burn the dog's skin.

Right before you start the bath, put about 1/8-inch (3-mm) ribbon of petroleum jelly on each corner of the dog's eyes. This will protect them from soapy water.

Technique

1. If you know how and plan to depress the anal sacs, you should do this first. Wear rubber gloves. Express the anal sacs into a triple-folded tissue or dry cotton. When you have cleaned out both sides, gently wipe the anus

BOSTON TERRIER

with another clean piece of cotton. Then fold the glove over the tissue or cotton and throw it away.

2. Set the temperature of the water so that it is warm to the touch, not hot. Wet either the facecloth or the sponge. Do not use soap yet.

3. Gently wipe your dog's face with the wet facecloth or sponge. Be sure to avoid getting water in the eyes, nose, ears, and mouth. If you get water in your dog's nose, he may panic.

4. Wet the dog's neck and work down his body until you get to the tail.

5. Take a small amount of dog shampoo and work it into the wet facecloth or sponge. Gently rub the soapy water into the hair on the dog's face, avoiding the eyes, ears, mouth, and nose. You can use your fingers to work up a bit of lather.

6. Work the shampoo down the neck onto the rest of the body. Be sure to soap the dog's belly, legs, and tail as well as his back.

7. Thoroughly rinse out the facecloth or sponge with clean water.

8. With the facecloth or sponge as wet as you can make it, gently dribble water on your dog's face as you wipe the soap away, but do not use so much water that it runs into his eyes, ears, nose, or mouth.

9. Using the hose spray or cup, rinse the rest of the dog, working from the top of the neck to the tail.

10. If you plan to shampoo your dog twice, repeat steps five through nine.

11. After you have finished rinsing your dog, run your soap-free hand over the dog's body to check that you have rinsed off all of the soap. Be sure to check his underside as well.

12. If you plan to use creme rinse, apply it to the dog's coat now. Work it in with your fingers, massaging the dog as you do so.

13. Let the creme rinse sit on the dog for about a minute, or as long as the directions state.

14. Now rinse your dog again if the directions for the creme rinse do not require that the rinse be left in the dog's coat.

15. Gently rub your dog's face with a towel. Continue to rub the dog dry until you have dried off his entire body.

MEDICAL CONSIDERATIONS

Before you bring your new pet home, you should have already chosen a veterinarian. Some of the criteria you can use to help you choose a veterinarian follow.

Choosing a Veterinarian

✔ Ask friends who own dogs how they like their veterinarians.

✔ Ask other professionals, such as your local groomer, dog trainer, boarding kennel operator, or pet shop to make recommendations.

✔ Go to all the nearby veterinary clinics, explain that you are getting a new dog, and ask to see the facilities and meet the doctor.

✔ Determine which clinic has hours that suit your schedule, and find out if it maintains 24-hour emergency coverage.

✔ If the clinic uses an emergency service, find out where it is located, as it may be too far away to be able to handle a real crisis situation for you.

✔ Ask each clinic how much the basic office visit costs, as well as some other charges, such as spaying and neutering, shots, teeth cleaning, and so on.

✔ Find out how many veterinarians work at the clinic. (You may prefer the security of knowing that a larger clinic is open longer hours and has someone on call, or you may opt for a smaller office where you always can be seen by the same person.)

An Ounce of Prevention...

There are many things you can do to keep your Boston Terrier healthy and happy. Accidents harm and kill more dogs each year than people realize. Just think of how many dead dogs you see lying along the roadside. Before you allow your Boston Terrier to engage in any activity, think of the many things that could possibly go wrong.

Playing off leash: Do not let your dog play off the leash near major roads or in areas adjacent to traffic unless the area is securely fenced. If the area in question is a public place, be sure to walk the fence line to look for any openings through which a small dog could escape. Even the most obedient dog will disobey occasionally, and all you need is one accident to ruin or even end your pet's life.

Swimming: If you want to allow your dog to try swimming, be sure that the water is safe.

You must consider the current, both on and under the surface. Even with a mild current, a Boston Terrier could easily be swept away. Unlike water dogs, such as Labrador Retrievers, Bostons are not strong swimmers. You must also be concerned about possible toxic substances in the water, as all dogs drink some water as they swim.

The woods: If you are going to allow your dog to run in the woods, be on the lookout for leg-hold traps that have been placed on animal runs. You should also carry a first aid kit to care for bee stings, snake bites, cuts, and scrapes.

If you are hiking in the woods in certain parts of the country, beware of old wells and holes into which a small dog could fall. By keeping your dog on a leash or in your sight, you will prevent most of these types of accidents from happening. Think before you allow your dog to do *anything*.

Toxic plants: Prevention should be the watchword for your home as well. Toxic plants occur inside and outside the home; be sure that all dangerous plants are out of chewing range for your dog. Check with your veterinarian, poison control center, or local extension agent to determine which toxic plants are found in your area. Even though young puppies are more likely to chew plants and chemicals than adults, an older dog can be counted on to occasionally chew something he should not. If your dog happens to eat a toxic plant, you should call your veterinarian or poison control center right away. Do not wait for symptoms to develop.

TIP

General Safety

Not for dogs! The following are either poisonous, toxic, or pose physical or mental threats.

Chocolate; raisins, grapes, candy, and gum; the artificial sweetener xylitol found in candy, gum, and baked goods; alcohol; macadamia nuts, onions, poultry bones, eggnog, nuts, spicy sauces, and dressings; potpourri; lilies, mistletoe, poinsettias; foil and cellophane; fertilizer, electric cords, fireworks, de-icing products, antifreeze; toys with ribbons or strings; items made in foreign countries that may have toxins in them. If you are in doubt, contact the ASPCA's Animal Poison Control Center at *http://www.aspca.org/* or (888) 426-4435.

Weed killers and fertilizers: If your dog should eat a plant that you are not sure of, take a sample of it to your local garden center for identification, or call your veterinarian. Bear in mind that weed killers can be much more harmful to dogs than the plants themselves. Also, be careful of fertilizers, both for outdoor and indoor use. Most chemical fertilizers are toxic to animals.

Boston Terriers, being small animals, are low to the ground and can breathe in significant quantities of weed killers and fertilizers. Dogs have been known to get sick from eating grass treated with liquid chemicals. Check with the manufacturer and your veterinarian before using any of these chemicals around your pet.

Poisons: Rodent poisons are another concern. While some require a number of ingestions to kill a dog, you should still call your veterinarian immediately if you suspect that your dog has eaten some.

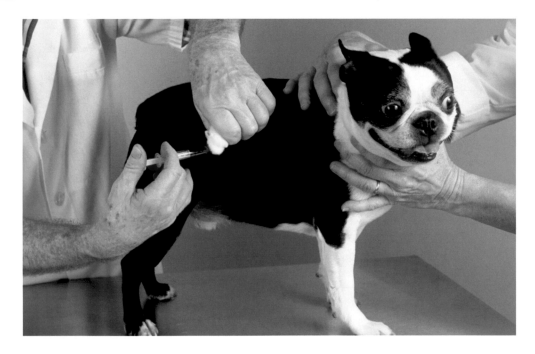

Immunizations

As a responsible owner, it will be important to properly take care of the health of your dog. Part of this care includes regular vaccinations. Timely inoculations can prevent many serious diseases, some of which can be deadly.

During the first year of your dog's life he will need to get a series of inoculations, after which regular boosters will keep your dog's immunity at an acceptable level. Your veterinarian will work out a schedule of inoculations based on your dog's health, age, and weight. Also be sure to discuss tick and flea control with your veterinarian.

If you live in an area where your dog will be walking on grass, or in woods or fields, you may want to consider a vaccination against Lyme disease (see page 62).

Some Serious Diseases

Canine distemper: Canine distemper is a highly contagious disease caused by a virus that can be spread in the air or through contact with infected dogs through respiratory secretions; however, it can be prevented with inoculations. Symptoms for this disease resemble the common cold in humans. The dog's eyes will be watery and his nose will run. Next, usually within days, the discharge will turn thick yellow. The dog will then develop a fever, become listless, and not want to eat. Seizures are late symptoms, and death frequently results. Sometimes a dog can appear to recover, only to experience a lethal relapse.

Distemper is not limited to dogs and can be found in other small mammals. The disease is often found in puppies, but adults can catch it too if they have not had their annual booster vaccinations. It is not unusual for a whole litter of puppies to die of distemper.

Leptospirosis: Leptospirosis is caused by species of the *Leptospira* bacteria. These spirochete are usually found in the urine of an infected animal. Your dog can become infected by drinking, swimming, or wading in infected water, and by eating infected food. Due to improved sanitation practices and widespread inoculation, this disease is no longer common. However, it can be transmitted to humans.

Signs include loss of appetite, fever, muscle weakness, vomiting, lethargy, abdominal pain, and kidney or liver failure. The dog can become jaundiced, weak in the hind legs, develop sores in the mouth, and suffer from abdominal pain.

Canine hepatitis: This is a highly contagious disease that usually strikes quickly. Although it can be mild, severe cases can cause quick death in dogs. If left untreated, the virus will attack the liver, kidneys, and the lining of the blood vessels.

The signs of hepatitis are listlessness, fever, tonsillitis, bloody stools, abdominal pain, and vomiting.

Canine parvoviral disease: Parvo is serious disease caused by a virus; however, it is easily prevented with a vaccine. It is very contagious and mainly attacks the gastrointestinal system. The symptoms are a fever, vomiting, and severe, often bloody, diarrhea. It is spread by direct contact between dogs as well as by contaminated stool, surfaces, bowls, collars, leashes, equipment, and the hands and clothing of people. It can also survive in the soil for years, making the virus hard to kill. This should be kept in mind when taking your dog to a dog park. It is essential to bring your dog to your

veterinarian immediately, since many dogs die from parvo despite intensive treatment.

Rabies: All warm-blooded animals, including humans, are susceptible to rabies. The disease is transmitted through the saliva of an infected animal. Rabies causes the brain to become inflamed, which will cause altered behavior and neurological function. Some of the signs are withdrawal, paralysis, and erratic violent behavior.

Rabies is endemic and widespread. Every year rabid animals are reported throughout the country. If you see a mammal of any species acting strangely, do not attempt to catch it yourself. Instead, call the proper animal-control authorities. They will catch the animal and either quarantine it to see if it develops rabies or else destroy it if symptoms become evident.

As long as your Boston Terrier is not exposed to wildlife (including mice) there is no great danger to either you or the dog. If your pet should be bitten by a wild animal, immediately call your veterinarian to treat the wound and take precautionary measures against rabies. Up-to-date vaccines, required for license renewal in most areas, are the best prevention.

Parainfluenza: Also known as kennel cough, this can be caused by a combination of viruses and bacteria. Because of its frequent appearance in group settings, the disease has been nicknamed "kennel cough." However, your dog can catch it just as easily from an encounter with a single infected animal.

Signs are a dry, hacking cough that, if left untreated, will be followed by retching to get rid of mucus in the throat. In and of itself, this disease is not life-threatening. The danger lies in increased vulnerability to other infections and ailments.

Your veterinarian can give your dog nose drops or a vaccine to prevent kennel cough. This is especially important if you frequent areas where your dog will mingle with other dogs, or if you plan to board your dog.

Lyme disease: Like rabies, Lyme disease can affect all warm-blooded animals, including humans. It is transmitted by the deer tick. Because these ticks are about the size of a pinhead, they are almost impossible to spot, making prevention the best course. If you live in an infested area, and you plan to walk, hike, or otherwise spend any amount of time outdoors with your dog, you should take precautions.

The symptoms of Lyme disease can vary from case to case. Many times, when your dog is bitten by an infected tick, the bite will swell, or there may be a painless red rash. However, the rash may not appear, or it can be small and easily missed. Later symptoms of Lyme disease can include arthritic swelling and tenderness of the joints. If treated right away, it is possible to cure the dog, but delay in treatment can lead to difficulties.

After your walk use a flea comb to check your pet. A good precaution for your dog is to use a topical flea and tick product, and get a Lyme vaccine.

Boston Terriers are at risk, either through injury or inheritance, to get the following:

Patellar Luxation: the kneecap slips out of position

Cleft palate: an opening in the roof of the mouth

Bilateral cataracts: opaque spots on the lens of the eyes

Epilepsy: seizure disorder

Brachycephalic syndrome and stenotic nares and elongated soft palate: difficulty breathing, especially in hot weather

Atopic dermatitis: a skin allergy triggered by dust mites, poor food, pollens

Mitral stenosis: weak mitral valve in the heart, which leads to an enlarged heart

Deafness: one or both ears

Corneal ulcer: caused by eye injuries and common in dogs with prominent eyeballs

Dry eye: inadequate tear flow, which leads to chronic infections

Cushings disease: usually a disease of older dogs, in which too much glucocorticoid is produced by the adrenal or pituitary glands

Pyloric stenosis: a narrowing of the opening in the small intestines

Hydrocephalus: excess spinal fluid built up in the brain, usually in very young puppies

Hemivertebrae: an unnatural angle of the spine causing it to twist and/or compress

Craniomandibular osteopathy: affects the bones of the jaw in dogs under ten months of age.

Internal Parasites

Dogs are afflicted by a number of species of parasitic worms. Almost all puppies have worms, and adult dogs can pick them up too.

Although a light infestation of worms is not usually evident, wormy puppies will not thrive. In both puppies and adult dogs, worms can cause serious health problems and death.

Some worms can be detected by microscopic examination of the feces, while others are found in the blood. In some cases you can actually see the worms around the dog's anus or in his stool.

You should never consider worming your pet without consulting your veterinarian. Worming medications are formulated for use against specific worms, so proper diagnosis is essential. Over-the-counter medications might not be effective against your pet's worms, and some can actually cause harm. The same is true of homemade worming preparations or remedies. Your first visit to the veterinarian with your puppy should include a stool or feces sample for the veterinarian to check. After that you should have your dog checked for worms at least twice a year—when he gets his annual booster shots, then six months later. To do this, take a fresh stool sample with you for examination. This will ensure that your dog is free of these pesky internal parasites. Mild infestations of all types of worms may not be evident right away; therefore, a regular checkup will keep your dog healthy.

If your dog should get worms, it is important to keep your living area and the places where the dog eliminates very clean, so that he will not become reinfected. Some worms are eliminated in the dog's stools, and will survive in the ground for a long time. Check with your veterinarian about the best way to disinfect your dog's toilet area.

As a general rule of thumb, you should look at your dog's stools daily when they are fresh to check for worms, blood, mucus, color, and consistency. Often this is the only way you can spot the early warning signs of disease or infestations in your dog.

Intestinal parasites such as roundworms, hookworms, whipworms, and tapeworms are transmitted in a similar manner. They lay eggs that are passed in the dog's stool and infect other dogs when they eat contaminated soil, lick contaminated fur or paws, or drink water contaminated with the stool from infected dogs. Tapeworms, on the other hand, are spread when dogs eat fleas, lice, or rodents infected with tapeworms.

All worms can cause malnutrition since they feed on the nutrients from the dog's food as it is digested. Worms can cause diarrhea, and hookworms can cause blood loss since they hook into the intestine of the dog and feed on blood.

Roundworms: These are most often found in puppies. Typically these are the worms that look like spaghetti, in that they are light in color, long, and round. They can be very visible to the naked eye.

Even though roundworms are common in puppies, if left untreated they pose a threat to the young and small puppy. A roundworm infection can cause pneumonia, inflammation of the lungs, and intestinal blockage. Roundworms can kill young puppies. Have your veterinarian examine the puppy to determine if he has worms.

Coccidia and giardia are single-celled parasites that damage the lining of the intestine. Dogs can become infected with coccidia by eating infected soil or licking contaminated paws or fur. Puppies are at the highest risk of infection and illness.

Heartworm: These round worms are parasitic on dogs, cats, and ferrets. The larvae are transmitted by mosquitoes and live under the dog's skin for two or three months. Then they mature into worms and travel through the bloodstream to the heart and lungs. They can live there for up to five years and grow from 4 to 12 inches (10–30 cm) long. They wrap themselves around the heart valves and can cause heart failure and death.

The effects of heartworm do not show until years after the initial infection. The major symptoms are a dry, soft cough and an inability to tolerate exercise. Later complications can involve the heart, liver, and kidneys.

Heartworm is one of the most easily preventable of canine diseases. If you live in a region where the disease is endemic, you can give your dog a daily or monthly preventive medication, which can be obtained from your veterinarian.

Hookworms: These can be present in both adult dogs and puppies. The eggs hatch into larvae, which attach themselves to the feet of the same or another dog and penetrate the skin. Larvae can also be swallowed with food, water, or even inhaled when a contaminated area is sniffed. As with roundworm infestation, puppies with a heavy infestation of hookworms will not thrive. The stool will be bloody or inky, the pups will not maintain their weight, and they may not eat well. If left untreated for a long period, hookworms can cause the development of scar tissue in the intestines, which will cause chronic intestinal problems for the rest of the dog's life. Because hookworms attach themselves to the intestinal wall and suck blood, your puppy can develop anemia and could die.

In clean surroundings hookworm infestation is rare. Therefore, breeders and owners should maintain meticulously sanitary conditions. However, if you walk your dog in areas where many animals have been (such as the exercise pen at a dog show), your pet can get hookworms regardless of how clean you keep your home area.

Tapeworms: Tapeworms are long, flatworms that can be acquired by many kinds of animals, including humans. They consist of a head, which attaches to the intestinal wall, and a large number of sections. Each section is filled with eggs and has the capacity to become a new tapeworm. When the segments are ready, they pass out of the dog in the stool.

There are several species of tapeworms, each with a different life cycle. Fleas are the principal intermediate host for the Dipylidium tapeworm in dogs. Fleas ingest the tapeworm eggs that have been passed in the dog's feces, and the tapeworm eggs develop into cysts inside the flea. If the flea jumps on a dog and the dog happens to swallow the flea, the dog becomes infected with the tapeworm. Farm animals such as sheep, cattle, and pigs can serve as intermediate hosts for the Echinococeus tapeworm. The farm animals get the tapeworms from grazing in areas infected by dog droppings, and the dogs get the tapeworm from eating the offal of an infected animal.

Although not life-threatening, tapeworms can cause general poor health in your dog. If a tapeworm is present, you will usually see segments hanging from the hairs around the dog's anus or in the stools. Sometimes the worm can pass in very long segments and appear as white or gray strings that your dog strains to eliminate. Your veterinarian, who can examine stool samples for tapeworm eggs, can also provide you with effective medication.

Whipworms: Generally, whipworms affect dogs over six months of age. Some dogs can

have whipworms with no side effects; others can develop foul-smelling diarrhea, which can become a problem.

Because whipworm eggs have a very thick shell, it is possible for them to lie dormant for years. This can make it very difficult to clean an infected area.

The larvae develop inside the egg and stay there until conditions are right for them to hatch. The dog picks up the eggs on his paws when he walks on contaminated ground. When the dog licks his paws, the eggs are ingested. They hatch in the small intestines, then move to the large intestines. Finally, they are passed with the feces, and the cycle starts all over again.

A dog can also pick up whipworm eggs if he eats contaminated dirt.

External Parasites

Fleas: These are perhaps the most troublesome of the external parasites. Fleas feed on the dog's blood and can cause anemia. They also transmit tapeworms. Some Boston Terriers can develop an allergic reaction to flea saliva, which will cause hair loss, constant scratching, and skin problems.

The best way to handle fleas is to prevent an infestation. Because Boston Terriers have short hair, it is fairly easy to spot the fleas. If you go over your dog every day with a flea comb, you should catch fleas before they have time to infest your dog and your house. If you see little black specks on your dog or on the flea comb, drop it into a small drop of water. If it turns blood red, it is the dropping from fleas. That means that your dog has fleas, even if you do not see one.

There are a number of products that you can get from your veterinarian to prevent fleas from becoming a problem. Some products sterilize the fleas so that they cannot reproduce, but do not kill the flea. Therefore, if your dog has a flea allergy, this may not be the best solution for your dog. Other products kill the fleas directly.

If your dog becomes severely infested, it may be a good idea to treat your house and yard as well. Consult your veterinarian or exterminator.

Ticks: These are also bloodsuckers, and certain species can transmit disease, including Lyme disease. Ticks usually do not attach themselves to your dog right away, so if you go out in areas that may be infested, check your dog as soon as you come home, and you may be able to pick off any ticks before they embed themselves in the dog.

If you find that a tick has attached itself to your dog, take it off as soon as possible. Clean the bite and apply a first aid cream.

To remove a tick, use special tick removal tweezers. Do not use alcohol or other products that try to kill the tick on the dog. If you do, the tick will regurgitate and infect the dog with any diseases it may carry. The tick tweezers gently lift the tick, causing it to release itself from the dog. Follow the directions on the package.

Once the tick is removed, kill it by placing it in a small amount of rubbing alcohol. Then put the body in a small plastic bag, or between two pieces of sticky tape such as masking tape and throw it away. Sticking the tick on tape will prevent it from crawling away if you did not kill it.

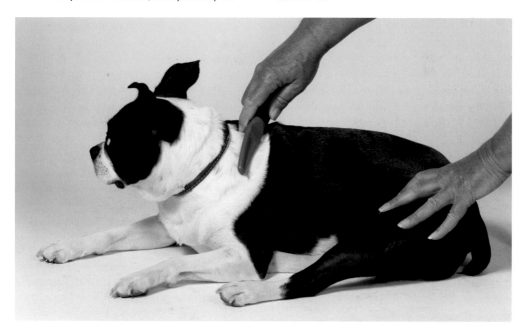

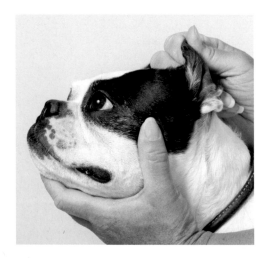

Ear mites: These parasites, which live in the ear canal, cause *otitis* (or ear inflammation) and produce a dark, waxy residue. Ear mites are transmitted from one animal to another. While they usually cannot be seen with the naked eye, you can notice a strong odor in the ear. Ear mites should be treated immediately by your veterinarian.

Mange: The two most common types of mange are *demodectic*, or red mange, and *sarcoptic* mange, or scabies. Both types are caused by mites. Red mange usually affects old dogs and puppies. The dog will suffer from hair loss and sometimes itching. Scabies is a highly contagious condition transmitted by physical contact. Humans can pick up the parasite as well. Scabies causes hair loss and very bad itching. You should take your dog immediately to a veterinarian for treatment.

Other skin problems: Boston Terriers can suffer from allergies to pollen, chemicals, flea bites, and so on, and contract fungal infections.

Your dog's body changes as he ages, and he may experience reactions to irritants that never bothered him before. If you notice symptoms such as bald spots, itching, rashes, scabs from scratching, or discharges, take your pet to your veterinarian immediately.

Other Illnesses and Medical Problems

Vomiting and diarrhea: There are a number of conditions that can cause these symptoms. Stress could be a cause, as well as eating grass, or any change in diet. Sometimes sudden hot weather can cause a dog to drink excessively, and this can result in one or two bouts of diarrhea or vomiting. Try withdrawing all food for 12 hours. Provide small amounts of fresh water. If the symptoms are relieved, offer a small quantity of food. However, if vomiting recurs, or if vomiting or diarrhea lasts longer than 12 hours, or if there are other signs of illness, call your veterinarian without delay.

Constipation: Lack of exercise can cause constipation, even if the inactivity is due to a long trip in a confined area. If it lasts longer then a day, or if the dog is in discomfort, call your veterinarian.

Epilepsy: Epilepsy is a condition of recurring seizures. Different types of seizures cause different symptoms, including loss of consciousness, collapse, muscle spasms, shaking, and loss of control of the bowels and bladder. The seizure itself may often be preceded by a period of altered behavior, which can include restlessness, pacing, an abnormal need for affection, heavy salivation and drooling, shivering or shaking, and hiding. During the seizure, the dog can exhibit excitement, vomiting, salivation, and running in circles, as well as the more severe behavior mentioned above.

If your dog has what you think is a seizure, try to remove anything nearby that could hurt him, such as furniture and sharp objects. Do not put your hand in the dog's mouth. If the seizure does not end within five minutes, call your veterinarian for emergency help.

Diabetes: This refers to a serious metabolic disease in which there is excess sugar in the blood, caused by a decrease in the amount of effective insulin in the body. While there is no cure, it can be controlled, sometimes by diet alone, although daily injections may be required. Some of the signs are an increase in appetite and hunger, and increased urination.

Pancreatitis: This is inflammation of the pancreas, usually occurring in overweight, middle-aged female house dogs that have lived on a high-fat diet. The signs include vomiting, diarrhea, lack of appetite, depression, restlessness, and tenderness of the stomach and belly. In some cases, proper medication and diet can keep a dog alive and comfortable with pancreatitis for a long time. Acute pancreatitis requires immediate veterinary care or it may become life-threatening.

Special Considerations for the Older Dog

From about eight years of age on, various aspects of your dog's physiological function will tend to become less efficient. With a little bit of care and extra precautionary measures, you can make sure your dog has a long, healthy, and comfortable life.

Perhaps the most important factor in producing a hale and happy old age for your dog is proper nutrition and health care.

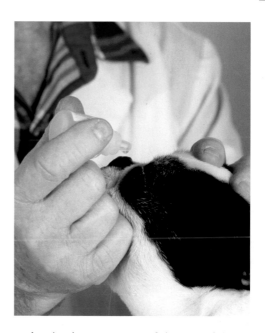

Another important part of the care of the older dog is to give him a complete veterinary examination every year. Depending upon your dog's condition and age, this should include an analysis of blood and urine. These tests will allow your veterinarian to discover problems in the early stages, before symptoms have become evident. They will reveal the state of function of the major organs in your dog's body, the presence of infection, and much more.

Arthritis is a common problem in older dogs. Many veterinarians can recommend non-drug supplements and an exercise program that can help your dog avoid the pain of arthritis. Acupuncture is another way to treat arthritic pain, as well as pain from other causes.

You should use these measures only under the direction of a veterinarian who is trained in their use. To obtain a list of licensed veterinary acupuncturists, see page 92.

HOW–TO: GIVE MEDICINE

Over the course of your dog's life, you may have to give your dog a pill or liquid medicines. This can be easy if you know how.

✔ Discuss the possibility of using a pill dispenser or syringe for liquid medicine. A pill dispenser is commonly used to give pills to cats, and can be handy to give a difficult dog a pill. Sometimes a syringe such as the type used to give human babies liquid medicine will work for a dog as well.

✔ Get all of your supplies and the medicine ready before you try to hold your dog.

✔ Either put the pill in a pill dispenser or hold the pill in the tip of your fingers. Tilt the dog's head back. Next, gently open the dog's mouth by inserting your finger in the side of his mouth and opening it just enough to place the pill as far back on the tongue as possible. If you are administering liquid medicine, you want to squirt it into the dog's mouth as far back as possible.

✔ Close the dog's mouth quickly and hold it closed. Sometimes gently rubbing the dog's throat in a downward motion helps the dog swallow the pill.

If taking medication is stressful to your Boston Terrier, he may become fearful of such attention. Considering the need for monthly heartworm preventive, such behavior can be very awkward. It may also be necessary to administer a topical medicine to your dog for fleas and ticks. If your dog is fearful, even this simple application may become difficult. The more your dog struggles, the greater the risk of injury. It may even result in your not giving the dog the medication needed. Teaching your dog to accept medications is fairly simple. Always reward your dog for taking the medication with a special treat your dog gets only at this time. This way, taking medications becomes a treat instead of a trial.

It will also help your dog enjoy or at least tolerate medication time if you administer them properly.

Giving Oral Medications

The checklist at the start of this section gives an overview of how to give oral medication. Your job will be easier and your dog will feel better if you hide the pill or liquid in something very tasty. Cheese, liverwurst, canned cat food, and human (meat) baby food work well. Add the liquid or

pill to a small morsel of the food and give it to your dog. If you must open the dog's mouth to put the pill in, do not wear jewelry that could cause injury. The same applies if your nails are so long that you risk cutting or scraping the dog's mouth. Also be very careful when grasping your dog's muzzle, that you do not pinch his nose and cut off his breathing. This will frighten your dog more than taking medications! Generally avoid touching your dog's nostrils.

Giving Eye Medications

Eye medications are usually in liquid or ointment form. When treating eyes, it is very important that you do not touch the eye itself with your hands or any applicator.

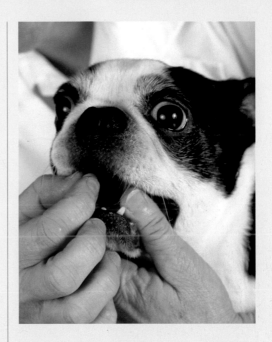

For both liquid and ointment, hold the applicator parallel to the eye. This will help avoid injury if the dog makes any sudden move. Hold the dog's head steady, since it is a natural reaction for your dog to pull away. Gently pull the lower eyelid down, squeezing a small amount of medication into the lower lid. Avoid putting any finger pressure on the part of the eyeball covered by the lower lid as you pull the eyelid down. Be sure the medication gets inside the lid instead of on the outside. It will not take much movement from your dog for you to miss the medication spot. You may need help holding the dog while you accomplish this action. After instilling the medication into the dog's eye, close the eye to spread the medication evenly.

Ear Medication

Ear medications are fairly easy to administer. Gently hold your dog's head steady. Hold the ear flap back to steady the ear. Apply the med-

ication into the ear canal if it needs to be in deeper or rub it on the surface structure. If the medication needs to be in the ear canal, gently rub the ear or massage the ear at the base to distribute the medication thoroughly.

You can apply a cotton ball to the ear before the dog shakes his head to prevent the medication from flying out. As soon as the dog stops shaking his head, remove the cotton ball.

Topical Medication

Topical or skin medications are the easiest of all to apply. Since this type of medication is often rubbed into the skin, be careful to rub as lightly as you can, especially if the area is sore. Be sure to apply the medication to the entire area that needs it, all the way to the edge. At all times, follow the instructions of your veterinarian exactly.

TRAINING YOUR BOSTON TERRIER

Be aware that there are almost as many methods of dog training as there are dog trainers. There is absolutely no need to use a method that employs punishment, inflicts pain, or is in any way harsh. You should never use choke collars, pinch collars, prong collars, or electric collars when training your Boston Terrier.

Getting Started

Never lose sight of the fact that training is actually a process of *teaching* the dog what *you* want him to do.

If you want your dog to learn something, make it meaningful to your dog. There are two main interactions between you and your dog that make anything meaningful to him. One is praise from you and the other is food. By associating either or both with an activity, it will become meaningful to your dog.

Most dogs are very eager and willing to please us if they understand what we want. Therefore, it is important to show exactly what you expect your dog to do.

Click and Treat Training

Although the following instructions are based on more traditional methods of positive dog training, the author strongly urges the reader to research and use the click and treat

method of dog training. There is much information about this method on the Internet and in books devoted to click and treat training.

Click and treat training will work with dogs of all ages. You need a device that will make a distinctive sound, such as a training clicker or another object that makes a distinctive noise. Some of the objects that are used to make noise are click pens that have a loud click, the tops of baby food jars, or any metal or plastic object that makes a noise when pressed.

Once you have your "clicker" you can start to condition the dog to it. You need a primary reinforcer, which is anything that the dog will work for, usually food or a favorite toy. The secondary reinforcer is the clicker. The clicker by itself is meaningless to the dog, but by coupling it with the primary reinforcer, it will become meaningful to the dog; thus you can shape the dog's behavior by using the click from the clicker, which is the secondary reinforcer. The secret to using this method of training is to understand when and how to apply it to the training situation. Dogs usually love it, and this method removes the need to correct the dog because wrong responses are not important. The end result is a dog that thoroughly enjoys working with you and responding to commands.

Training Rules

Training is carried out by means of repetitive exercises. The dog is taught to perform certain actions in response to specific cues given by you. The cues come in three categories:

1. what you say (the *command*)
2. how you say it
3. the movements you make

Remember that dogs do not speak English; therefore, *how* you say it will mean more than *what* you say, and what you *do* will be more important still.

It is also important to follow a few simple rules when training a dog.

1. Be consistent in your actions as well as your commands. You cannot call a dog to come to you by using the word "*Come*" one time and "*Here*" the next. When you call your dog, you cannot let him walk to your side one time and sit in front of you the next, and so forth.

2. Give a command once. Do not tell your dog "*Sit*," for example, three or four times. If you do this you are actually teaching the dog that (a) he does not have to listen to you right away, and/or (b) he does not have to listen to you at all.

3. Be fair. You should not punish your dog. Suppose someone put an advanced calculus problem on a piece of paper, told you "This is a math problem. Do it!" and then slapped you when you did not solve it immediately. How would you feel? This is exactly what some training methods do to a dog.

4. Praise or correct immediately. Dogs associate praise or correction with what they are doing *at that moment*. If your pet chews on something, then walks over to you and you give correction, he will assume that you are correcting him for coming to you. You cannot explain that you are actually angry with the dog for chewing.

5. Ask your dog to work only as long as he is able. The younger the dog, the shorter the training session. The longest session for any dog should be about ten minutes. Also, give serious consideration to the weather conditions at the time of training. Boston Terriers cannot tolerate hot, humid weather. It would be unreasonable to ask your dog to work for you if the weather is uncomfortable.

6. Ask your dog to do only as much as he can understand. Again, the younger the dog, the smaller the request. If you have not taught your dog to understand you, he will become confused. Training is teaching.

7. Set up your training sessions so that the dog can win. Your pet will gladly respond to you if he is praised for doing the exercise correctly. You should always praise and reward your dog, even if it means that you have to set things up so that he wins.

8. Train your dog before his main meal, or two to three hours or more after the main meal. Few people (and dogs) want to go out and exercise right after they eat a big dinner. You will find your pet much more responsive if you let him digest his food first, or if you have your session before the meal.

9. Make sure that everyone who comes in contact with your dog uses *your* commands. It is very difficult for a dog to understand what you, or anyone else, expects him to do if you use different words for the same command. An example of this would be if different people used the commands "*Lie down,*" "*Down,*" "*Rest,*" or "*Get*" when the dog is supposed to lie down.

10. Be sure to match your tone of voice with the command. You should try to sound enthusiastic and upbeat. Your dog will be more willing to interact will a bright, happy person than a grouch. If you are always harsh with your dog, he may come to fear you. It is much more enjoyable to have a dog that enjoys working *with* you.

11. Think like a dog. Of course, no one knows for sure just how a dog thinks, though scientists have developed some very interesting theories. One thing, however, seems clear. What is important and meaningful to humans is not necessarily important and meaningful to dogs. For example, dogs can see much better at night than humans; therefore, they never need a light outside in the dark. No matter how many times a dog watches humans turn on a light switch, he will not learn to do this on his own, because he sees no benefit to himself in having the light on. (When dogs are trained to assist the handicapped, they are taught to turn on light switches on command. But they will not do it on their own.)

12. Do not punish your dog. Encourage the behaviors you want, rather than punishing those you do not want. Many people fall into the trap of correcting their dogs for not following their commands, rather than praising when their pet performs properly. Your dog expects praise for doing something good. He

will not assume that your silence *also* means that he performed correctly. You must praise what is correct for the dog to understand which behavior is the one you want.

13. Each dog has a favorite activity or object. It may be a game or a toy. Most dogs have a number of foods they dearly love. All of these positive things can be used as rewards for the behavior you want to encourage.

unpleasant result to a given undesirable activity. Negative reinforcement is something the dog can stop simply by stopping undesirable behavior. An example is the choke chain. As the dog pulls, the choke chain chokes the dog. As soon as the dog stops pulling, the choke chain stops choking the dog. There is never a need to use negative reinforcement. Some dog trainers use this term to mask painful corrections.

16. Always give "*Start exercise*" and "*End exercise*" commands. Many people do not use these commands. They assume that the dog will understand when the lesson is to begin or to end, but this is not the case.

It is especially important to give an *End exercise* signal. This command should be used only when the training session is over, not after each step.

Here is an example of what can happen if you do not use an *End exercise* command. You tell your dog to "*Sit-stay,*" and walk away, forgetting about the dog. Theoretically, the dog should sit forever, but he will not. At some point the dog will break the *sit-stay*. What happens then is that the dog learns that you really do not mean what you say, or that he can break the command when he feels like doing so. When you give your dog choices, he will often make choices you cannot accept.

When you choose a *release* command, try to pick a word that is not commonly used. "*Okay*" is fine if you do not use it a great deal in your everyday language. "*Finished,*" "*Done,*" and "*End*" are all words you can use. The word itself is not important because dogs do not speak English. What is crucial is that you use the same word each time.

14. Corporal punishment should never be used. Use of such punishments as leash jerks, hitting, electric shock, or other unpleasant things can cause your dog to become afraid of you.

15. Negative reinforcement is not the same as punishment. It is an instant and consistent

17. Do not play during training sessions. This is important because the dog must not confuse the casual interaction you have together during play and the serious relationship that you should have during work.

18. Keep a record of your progress. It is not unusual for a dog to reach a plateau where it seems that no gains are made. You can become discouraged at these times and forget how much you have accomplished. If you keep a record of how you and your dog do, you will realize during the frustrating times that you have made quite a bit of progress.

Equipment

You will need a few pieces of equipment in order to train your dog.

✔ A 6-foot (1.8-m) leash, made of nylon webbing, leather, or canvas. You should not use a rope or chain leash.

✔ A collar that goes around the dog's neck. For very young puppies either a buckle-type collar or a martingale nylon collar can be used. The martingale collar can also be used for adult dogs. The neck collar is the one that stays on the dog at all times.

✔ Another very good training device is a head harness. This appliance can be very useful if used properly. With a small modification, most head harnesses can be used on a Boston Terrier. You can purchase a head harness at your local pet-supply store.

✔ Treats. These should be of a consistency that can be handled easily, as well as cut up into very small, 1/4-inch (6-mm) pieces. Use treats as a teaser that the dog will work harder to get more of, not as a meal that your dog has to sit and eat. Treats are used as a reward, not as a bribe.

Basic Commands

Following is a list of the basic commands you should teach your dog, along with exercises with which to teach them.

Sit: The purpose of this exercise is to teach your pet to sit on command. Place the dog on your left side. Gently take up the slack in the leash while you guide the dog's hindquarters down to the ground, simultaneously telling him "*Sit.*" If you use a head harness, gently tilt the dog's head back, guide the hindquarters down, and give the verbal command "*Sit.*" Another method is to hold a treat over the dog's nose and very slowly move it back over the dog's head. Most dogs will sit with this method. As soon as the dog sits, give him the treat.

As soon as the dog's hindquarters rest on the ground, praise him verbally and give him a pat on the head. Do not allow the dog to wiggle around while in the *sit* position. If he does this, gently reposition him, and give praise as soon as he becomes quiet.

Do not ask your dog to sit for very long, especially at the beginning of training. Sometimes, in the early sessions, you may have only a few seconds to give praise. A ten-second *sit* is a fair length of time for starters. Be sure to watch closely and praise immediately when your dog gives you a nice, quiet *sit*. As soon as you accomplish your goal, give the dog permission to get up. As your pet begins to get the idea, you can ask him to sit for longer periods of time—up to one minute—and to sit in the exact position you wish.

Walk with Me or Walk: Either of these is the command you give your dog when you want to go for a casual walk in the park. The dog is allowed to have the full leash, and to walk anywhere he wants to within the range of the leash. This means he can walk in front of you or behind you, can stop, or do whatever he wants, as long as he does not break the rules of the exercise. The rules are simple: the dog cannot lead, and he cannot pull.

To begin, give the command and start to walk. If your dog pulls, very gently change direction as you call his attention to the fact that you are doing so. This is how it works: As you are walking, your dog starts to forge ahead of you and pull. Abruptly, without hesitation, change direction while saying "*Hup! Hup! Hup! Walk.*" You cannot stop and wait for your dog, because he will then learn that if he pulls, you will stop while he strains to sniff an interesting smell.

As soon as he starts to walk in your direction without pulling, praise your dog as if he has performed a miracle.

After a few days of this you will be amazed at how your dog will pay attention to you and watch where you go. If you use a head harness you will find that the dog will give in sooner and walk much better. This is because every time you change direction, the dog's head will follow you. As soon as this happens, you can praise the dog for paying attention to you.

It is very important to not jerk the dog with a head harness or any other kind of collar. You can seriously injure the neck and spine. This is especially true with puppies.

Heel: The purpose of this exercise is to teach your dog to walk quietly by your side without pulling. While "*Walk with me*" is used for casual walking, "*Heel*" is the at-attention-and-behave command. It is usually used when you are in a crowded area and you want to be sure that your dog is safely by your side. It is also used for obedience trials.

It is a proper *heel* position when your dog sits quietly by your left side, his right shoulder even with your left leg. To do this, position your dog in that manner and tell him "*Sit.*" With the dog in *heel* position, first get his attention by calling his name, and, about one second later, give the command "*Heel*" as you start walking with your left leg. Encourage your dog to walk with you by sounding upbeat or slapping your leg.

When the dog starts to walk with you, praise him with a pat on the head and a hearty "*Good dog.*" After heeling for about a minute, stop and give a *sit* command.

As your Boston Terrier learns what you want, he will sit automatically when you stop. If he is reluctant to *heel* with you, do not drag him along, but rather, encourage the dog to follow you. Be sure to praise him each time he *heels* the way you want, even if only for a few seconds. Dog training is accomplished moment by moment!

Stay: To teach your Boston Terrier to *stay* you must be sure that the dog knows how to *sit*. Place the animal at your left side in *heel* position. Firmly hold the dog in place by the leash, simultaneously giving a firm *stay* command. Immediately leave the dog, starting off with your right foot. At the same time bring the palm of your left hand down in front of the dog's face. Step away from the dog, turning as soon as you are in front of the dog so as to face him.

Keep eye contact and watch for any attempt to get up. If the dog does attempt to get up, gently tell him "*Sit*" and "*Stay*" again. If he does get up, simply reposition your dog and start over. If you use a head harness you can keep the dog's head from going down, which discourages him from getting up.

Ask the dog to *stay* for only about ten seconds, then return to his side in *heel* position. To properly return to the dog, walk toward him, keeping your left side closest, and then

continue around behind him until you are again in *heel* position. Gradually, as the dog learns to *stay*, you can walk to the end of the 6-foot (1.8-m) leash and increase the staying time to one minute. Once you have accomplished this, you have taught your dog the *sit-stay*.

Recall: Once the dog has mastered the *stay* command you can teach him to come when called. Put the dog in a *sit-stay* position and leave, going to the end of the 6-foot leash. After waiting one minute, give the dog a very happy-sounding "*Come.*" You can clap your hands or open your arms wide, inviting your dog to rush to you.

As soon as he reaches you, give a *sit-stay* command, making sure that your pet stops right in front of you. As soon as he does, give the dog a lot of praise.

There is one thing you must never do. If your dog does something that displeases you, and then comes to you, never, *never* scold or otherwise show anger toward him. The dog will not understand that you are angry at him for something he did 20 minutes ago "over there." The only thing your dog will learn is to never come to you when you call. It takes a long time to regain a dog's trust once you lose it.

As your dog learns to come on command, you can use a longer leash to make him come from further away. You should also practice this exercise in as many different places as you can, so the dog can learn to come to you no matter where you are.

Down: To teach your dog to lie down on command, you should first put him in a *sit-stay* position. It will be easier to teach this command if one end of your dog is already down.

Stand next to your pet in the *heel* position. With the dog in a solid *sit-stay*, gently run your right hand down the front of his face, so that his eyes will follow your hand to the ground. As you do this, gently pull down on the leash. If you are using a head harness, pull down and a little away so that the dog's head is guided to a spot about 6 inches (15 cm) in front of his feet, to give the dog a feeling of going down.

In some cases the animal will not get the idea to follow your hand into a *down* position. If this happens, you can use a treat to lure him into a *down* position. If you use one, you must be careful not to hold the treat so far in front

of the dog that the dog wants to get up to go after it.

You should constantly encourage your dog to go down, and praise him if any attempt is made to move toward the ground.

Once he is in a *down* position, tell him to *stay*. After a few seconds give a *sit* command, followed by a *release*. At this point, praise your dog some more.

As your dog gets the idea and learns to lie down on command, you can increase the time the dog stays down up to three minutes. Be sure to return to your dog after each *down* exercise and give the *release* command.

Go to Heel: This exercise is used to finish off the *recall* exercise. First, you must put your dog in a *sit-stay* position. Next, call him to you using the *recall* command. When the dog is sitting quietly in front of you, give the "*Go to heel*" command. At the same time, take a small step backward, just to get your dog moving, and lead him to your right side, around the back of your body, and into the *heel* position on your left. The dog should finish this exercise in *heel* position by your left side.

All of your obedience exercises should be practiced every day until the dog listens to you in a reliable manner. Since he will be expected to listen and obey no matter where you are, you should practice your obedience exercises in different places. Practice in town, in the country, in the park, in your home, in your backyard, at playgrounds, at shopping malls, and so on. Always remember when training your dog outside to check the weather. You should not practice outside in the heat of a summer day, nor should you make your dog walk on surfaces, such as blacktop, which are too hot. Remember that Boston Terriers have difficulty in the heat.

Obedience Classes

It is a very good idea to take your Boston Terrier to obedience class, or your puppy to puppy kindergarten. There are a number of options available.

✔ You can enroll your dog in a class offered by a local dog trainer, or by a dog-training club. These usually consist of about 10 to 20 other dogs and owners, and typically meet once a week. You will actually teach the dog yourself under the guidance of the trainer.

✔ Another possibility is to have private sessions with a trainer, who will tailor the sessions to your dog's abilities. You will be responsible for daily practice sessions.

✔ Some kennels offer the option of boarding your dog while having him trained for you. If you decide this is the way to go, be sure to check the facility and its reputation carefully. Since you will not be there, you will never be certain of the treatment your dog receives. (This is the least desirable way to train your pet. Participating yourself allows an opportunity to form a special bond with your Boston Terrier. It can also be great fun for the two of you.)

The Problem Dog

Unfortunately, even with the best of training and care, a dog can develop undesirable behaviors. There are many factors that can help to produce misbehavior, the most important of which are the dog's temperament and the inadvertent training of undesirable routines.

A dog's temperament, which is formed out of his inherited mental health plus reactions to his upbringing, can cause him to react negatively in certain situations.

It is also possible to teach your dog unfortunate habits, often without even noticing that you are doing so. Many times people will do things with their dogs to satisfy their own needs and communicate an altogether different message to the dog. Established undesirable behaviors can usually be corrected with a little patience and know-how.

Aggression Toward Owners

Although this is not a common problem with Boston Terriers, it does happen on occasion. Aggression toward owners should not be mistaken for a puppy's play and mouthing. It usually occurs in older dogs, although younger animals can display aggression as well. A growl toward an owner should be considered aggression, especially if it seems intended to precede a bite.

The owner can bear some of the responsibility for producing an aggressive dog. Some of the factors that trigger aggression are scolding and punishment.

If your dog bites you in a hostile manner, it is normal to feel as though your dog has betrayed you. In many cases, people who have been threatened or bitten by their dog will not have the same level of confidence when working with him in the future, and can even become afraid of their pet.

The first step in dealing with a dog that has shown aggressive behavior is to *stop all physical punishment*. Most dogs bite because they feel threatened. If you physically attack your dog you will make him feel more defensive. Remember that you appear overwhelmingly gigantic and powerful to your Boston Terrier.

You should not use *"Time Out"* as a punishment either. Many people think that if they put their dog outside, he will sit alone and feel bad, but this is not so. Putting the dog outside may actually be a reward if the dog likes to be outside.

If your dog should show aggression, immediately consult with a certified canine behavior consultant. There are different types of aggression, and diagnosing the problem is half the job. Never try to treat aggression yourself, nor should you use a dog trainer for this purpose. (See IAABC on page 92.)

Carsickness

Carsickness can be caused by stress. When a puppy is taken from his siblings for the first time, he is usually taken into a car right away—a major negative association. Lack of early socialization and handling can also make a puppy insecure in a car.

Carsickness often results when a bossy dog feels as though he is out of control of his environment. Obedience training will help.

The best cure for car sickness is to get your dog to associate fun with the car. Start by letting the dog get into the car when it is parked. Give the command to get into the car, and as soon as your dog does this, praise him and let him have a favorite toy. Then immediately let the dog get out of the car. Repeat this process over several days, until you see your dog eagerly jump into the car when you give the command.

Over several more days, lengthen the time the dog spends in the car. Finally, take short trips, gradually lengthening them. At the end of the process your pet should be able to ride in the car without stress.

Chewing

All dogs chew, and there is no point in trying to stop them. The best you can do is to teach them which items can be chewed and which can't.

Chewing in puppies is second nature and a part of growing up. Young puppies chew to explore their environment and to learn. Because they do not have hands as we do, dogs use their mouths to manipulate and hold things. It is our job to teach them which things are off limits for them.

There are some preventive steps you can take with your puppy to avoid a chewing problem. First, never give him old clothing of any kind to play with. How do you expect him to understand or to tell the difference between his old clothing and your new clothing? Never give your puppy leather toys or chews either. Again, the puppy can mistake your good leather products for the toys. Do not give him sticks to play with. Not only are they unsafe, but you will

encourage your puppy to chew everything in your house made of wood.

Chewing is a way to relieve stress. Avoid excited departures when you plan to leave home for a period of time, and try to ignore your puppy (until he settles down) upon your return. Being excited only increases your pet's stress when you leave. If your dog does chew something while you are away, do not pay attention to the mess when you come home. Clean it up when the dog does not see you doing it.

If your pet persists in chewing certain objects around your house, you can give those objects an unpleasant taste by spraying them with one of the many anti-chew products on the market, such as Bitter Apple. You can also use some of the stronger mouthwashes, such as Listerine.

Persistent, destructive chewing is usually a symptom of an underlying problem. If this describes your dog, you should consult an animal behaviorist.

Fearfulness

Dogs can be fearful of many things in life, and it is a sad thing to see a little Boston Terrier that is abnormally timid. Often, an owner's frightened response to some event will cause the dog to become even more fearful. If your dog reacts to the loud pop of a fire-cracker, for instance, he may recover from the noise without incident. But if you, or another human, get upset and call attention to the event, you may actually be teaching the dog to get upset as well.

The best thing you can do when a dog is fearful is to ignore the situation. Do not try to comfort him. The dog will misunderstand your action as praise for behaving in a fearful manner.

The first thing you must establish is that you are the dog's leader. This will allow him to follow your example. You should make your pet earn all affection and petting. Do not spoil your dog by petting him excessively; nor should you treat him in an unusually harsh manner.

Once you see that your dog is responding positively to you, you are ready to re-create the frightening situation. Set the stage to reenact the fearful event, using whatever props are appropriate, and be sure to have your pet's favorite toy on hand as well. Then bring your dog into the picture.

As you start enacting, start a play game with the dog. The goal is to get the dog to associate a happy activity with the fearful one. Soon the dog will look forward to the situation as an opportunity to play, rather than as something to be afraid of. You can do this exercise a few times a day. If the dog is very fearful or if you do not feel confident working with the problem, consult a canine behaviorist.

Submissive Urination

When a dog or puppy wets as he is approached by a human or animal, he does not realize he is urinating; therefore, you should not scold your pet for doing this. Correction will only make the problem worse and more difficult to cure. Submissive urination is part of very early puppy behavior, and is normal from birth until weaning. The mother dog initiates the behavior as part of the cleaning process for the puppies.

Usually, as the puppy grows up the submissive urination stops. If he does not, here are a few tips you can use to cure the problem.

First, take careful note as to when this occurs. Is it when you talk to the dog, come home, lean over him, and so on? Make sure that during such times you do not approach or act toward the dog in a threatening manner, but rather act very friendly and welcoming.

Sometimes you will need to avoid eye contact with the dog, or crouch down and let him come to you. You may also have to avoid talking to your dog as you approach him. Be sure to enlist the help of other people with this cure so that the dog is not submissive to all people.

If changing your attitude toward the dog does the trick, be sure to give the dog time to gain confidence.

Jumping on People

Often, puppies will rise up onto their hind legs, wanting to be picked up. It is one of their ways of letting you know they want attention. As a dog gets older this reaching up can become jumping up. Even though the reason, craving for attention, is the same, what seemed cute in a puppy is often unacceptable in an adult. Mature dogs that exhibit this behavior have been rewarded for it since puppyhood by being petted and receiving attention.

If you are wearing old clothes, and if you are a dog lover, you may not mind your dog jumping up. But if you have on good clothes you will not be happy. Guests in your house will

⎯BOSTON PERSONALS⎯

Sam Anderson says, "A Boston Terrier knows no other place to lie than on you. It has to be touching you. Boston Terriers are the gentlemen of the dog world. Every Boston I have owned goes behind you down the stairs, never in front. They always wait for you. Boston 'Terrorists' are con artists. They will figure out ways to con you to get their way. They will pretend to have to 'go,' run out, and then run back in and go right to the cookie jar. On laundry day, watch those piles of clothes and blankets—there is surely a Boston buried in one. Bostons love to kiss everyone, even the judges in the show ring. Bostons Terriers love all veggies. They will dig up your potatoes after you plant them. Bostons think they are as big as a Saint Bernard. Bostons are adorable puppies, clever as teenagers, and wise and gentle as seniors.

"Years ago a friend of mine was dying of cancer. Since he loved dogs but never owned one, we let him take care of Gidget while we traveled. Gidget never left his side and laid on the floor by his bed, a constant source of comfort."

almost always mind it if a dog jumps on them, even if it is a cute Boston Terrier. And although Bostons are not large enough to knock an adult over, they can cause a child or an elderly person to stumble and fall.

If you truly enjoy having your dog jump on you, then you should teach the dog to do this only on command. This way, the dog can be invited to jump when you desire it, rather than whenever he gets the urge.

There are two kinds of jumping. The type described above is friendly jumping and is the kind of good-natured physical contact the dog desires with humans. The second type of jumping is more assertive and pushy. Usually you can recognize this by the dog's attitude, and also by the fact that if you do not stay still, the dog will become more physical and may become upset, jumping with more determination. The assertive jumper is usually aggressive in other areas of interaction as well.

The best way to cure a jumping dog is to teach him to do something else when he feels the urge. To do this, you must first teach the dog to obey the *sit-stay* and *come* commands. If you see the dog coming in your direction and you have enough time, give the dog a firm *come* command. A dog that has been trained in the *come* command should approach and sit in front of you. Super praise from you is in order. If your dog does not do this, give him a firm *sit-stay* command, and gently guide him into position. Praise the dog when he relaxes into a sitting position in front of you.

If you do this every time the dog tries to jump, it should take only a few weeks for him to learn to sit instead of jump. Be sure to instruct your friends and guests not to allow your dog to jump. Well-meaning dog lovers can undo in minutes what it took you and your dog weeks to achieve.

The Overprotective Dog

A dog can become overprotective toward almost anything, including you.

Sometimes you may have brought on overprotectiveness in your pet through the

messages you have sent him. For example, if you feel threatened and fearful, especially of strangers, you may have praised the dog for showing protective behavior. Since your pet cannot make the same types of judgments as you, his protective behavior can rapidly develop into a problem situation in which he will go after any stranger who comes to your home. Sometimes a dog will become overprotective because of the owner's general insecurity in his or her relationship with the dog. In both cases the way to deal with it is the same.

✔ First, you must assume a leadership role. The dog must *earn* all praise and attention from you.

✔ Next, you should start a socialization program, similar to that for puppies (see page 35). You must show your dog how to behave by acting friendly toward people.

✔ Sometimes it will help if you have people give a small treat to your dog when he goes up to them. You can also bring along a special ball or toy that strangers can use to play with him. Generally, you will want the dog to learn that strangers are not to be feared.

Many people will wonder if the dog will protect them in the event of an intruder in the home. Socializing a dog will not lessen his protective abilities at all. On the contrary, the dog that knows which situations are acceptable and which are not will be a better protector. The dog will be much happier without all the worry associated with his need to protect you from everyone who comes along.

If your dog's overprotectiveness has progressed to the point where he has actually bitten someone, you have a problem on your hands. Consultation with a canine behaviorist is definitely indicated.

Barking

Sometimes a dog will bark excessively—both in the house and outside. A typical response to a barking dog is to yell at him to be quiet. But unless you teach your dog what the command "*Quiet*" means, the dog may think that you are just barking too. After all, if you take away the meaning of the English word "*Quiet*" as it is generally yelled at a barking dog, what does it sound like?

Before getting into the cure for barking, you should first consider *why* the dog is barking. Is it because the dog is alone, bored, frustrated, being teased? If any of these is the cause of the barking, your best bet would be to remove the cause. Often this will be enough to solve the problem.

If your dog barks at appropriate times but just a little too much for your taste, you can

train him to bark only within the limitations you set. First, teach him to speak on command. To do this, tease your dog with food and give a "*Bark*" command until he gives a frustrated bark. Immediately reward the dog with the food.

Once you have your dog barking on command, you can give him the command "*Bark*," followed by the command "*Quiet*." As you say "*Quiet*," extend your hand with a treat. Your dog cannot bark and sniff at the same time. As soon as he stops barking, praise your dog and give him the treat. Your dog will soon learn to stop barking when you say "*Quiet*."

Rooting in the Trash

This can be a frustrating problem. The dog gets to eat what he finds in the garbage, so the trash acts as his own reward. If you catch and scold your dog, he may learn to stay out of the trash when you are around, but may jump back in the minute your back is turned.

To cure a dog from going in the trash, you must make the trash punish the dog. Although mousetraps are a popular remedy for this problem, they can hurt and even cause damage. A better way is to blow up a balloon and put it on the top of the trash. As the dog goes into the trash, the balloon will pop loudly and the dog will find that the trash is not as nice as he thought. After a few tries the dog will give up making forays into your garbage.

Some Cute Tricks to Teach Your Boston Terrier

There are few things quite as delightful as seeing a dog perform tricks. The dogs love the attention and enjoy pleasing you. If your pet learns some tricks, you can entertain children, or even the elderly and shut-ins at a nursing home. A dog that performs simple tricks can bring a great deal of joy into many people's lives.

Before you start to teach your dog tricks, be sure that he is physically able to perform them. Each dog is different, and some may have difficulty where others may not. This is the most enjoyable form of dog training, and both you and your dog should have fun.

Always use a *release* word (see page 76) to let your dog know that the training session is over. And have a ready supply of treats on hand. Remember, treats should be a tease and not a meal. The ideal size is a pellet ¼ inch (6 mm) square.

Your dog should already be competent at all the basic commands. Of course, the very first step is to get the dog to pay attention to you when you speak to him. "*Come*" is a good exercise for this. By teaching your dog to come when you call, you will reinforce him for paying attention to you. The next important command is "*Sit-stay.*" You must be able to hold your dog's attention as well.

Go to a Particular Spot: This is the basis for many of the tricks you will want your pet to learn. Set up a small platform for him to sit on. The platform must be low enough so that your dog can easily get up on it. It must also be stable, and not move around under the dog. A small foot bench with a rug stapled to it will work well for the Boston Terrier.

With your dog on a leash and sitting in front of you, point to the bench and give the command as you do so. The command can be any word you choose to use, such as "*Up.*" Simultaneously, gently lead your dog to the platform and place him up on it. As soon as your pet is up, praise him and give him a treat.

Practice until your dog will go onto the platform on command.

Shake Hands: Give your dog a *sit-stay* command. Reach down, grab a paw, and hold it out as if you are shaking it. At the same time, give the command "*Shake hands.*" Do not pump the paw up and down until the dog knows the trick. As you are holding the dog's paw, reward him with verbal praise and a treat.

Saying Prayers: You will need a platform or a small stool, just high enough to allow your dog, when seated, to rest his front paws on the platform. Sit your pet in front of the platform. As you give the command "*Say your prayers,*" place the dog's paws on the stool while the dog remains in a sitting position. Immediately hold a small piece of treat between your dog's paws in such a way that your dog must place his nose between his paws to get the treat. Keep the dog in that position for a few seconds and then say "*Amen*" and allow your dog to get up.

By practicing this exercise your dog will learn to walk over to the stool, place his paws on the top of the stool, and hold his nose over his paws until you say "*Amen.*"

Sit Up: To teach your dog to sit up, you can use either a stick or the corner of a wall for support. Place your dog in a *sit-stay* position. Next, help him sit up by raising both of his front paws. As the dog holds this position, give him a treat and praise.

Balancing Food: Put your dog in a *sit-stay* position. Gently but firmly hold his nose in the palm of your hand. With your other hand, place a small piece of food on the tip of your dog's nose. Hold his nose so that he cannot get the food, and give the command "*Wait.*" Then give a *release* command and let go of his nose.

Generally, the dog will learn, after a number of tries, to flip the food into the air and catch it.

Take a Bow: While your dog is standing, place one of your arms around his belly in a hugging position. Your other hand is placed on top of his head. Gently lower the front half of the dog toward the ground, with the front legs extended and the head lowered, simultaneously giving the command "*Take a bow.*" Hold the dog in this position for a second as you reward him. Then give a *release* command and lots of praise.

Play Dead: Put your dog in a *sit-stay* position and then into a *down-stay*. Next, as you give the command "*Play dead,*" gently push the dog over onto his side and hold him in that position for a few seconds. Then give the *release* command, followed by praise. As the dog gets the idea, increase the amount of time you make him stay in the *play dead* position, so that the dog learns not to get up until told to do so.

Crawl: Find an object that is just tall enough for your pet to crawl under, such as a footstool. Place the dog on one side of the object and give a *sit-stay* command. Then go to the other side of the object. Give the *down* command, then call your dog and encourage him to come to you by crawling under the object. When he starts to do the right thing, give the command "*Crawl.*" Repeat this until your dog learns to go down and crawl toward you on command. Gradually raise the height of the object until your pet will crawl on the floor without needing an object to crawl under.

Organizations

To find the latest address, phone number, and web sites for the organizations listed, check the Internet.

American Kennel Club
260 Madison Avenue
New York, NY 10016

ASPCA Animal Poison Control Center
1717 S. Philo Road, Suite 36
Urbana, IL 61802
(888) 426-4435
www.apcc.aspca.org

Boston Terrier Club of America
Contact the American Kennel Club for the current address (which changes every two years).

Delta Society—Assistance Dogs, Therapy Dogs
(numerous locations)

Flying Disc Organizations:
Skyhoundz
International Disc Dog Handlers Association
U.S. DiscDogs
The Quadruped
     Canine Frisbee Disc Long Distance
          Catching Competition
     United Frisbee Dog Operations

IAABC International Association of Animal
     Behavior Consultants
www.IAABC.org

International Veterinary Acupuncture Society,
     Meredith L. Snyder, VMD
2140 Conestoga Road
Chester Springs, PA 19425
You may write to Dr. Snyder for a list of licensed veterinary acupuncturists.

Therapy Dogs Inc.
P.O. Box 5868
Cheyenne, WY 82003
www.therapydogs.com

United Kennel Club
100 E. Kilgore Road
Kalamazoo, MI 49002-5584

United States Department of Agriculture
(301) 436-7833

Books and Articles

American Kennel Club. *The Complete Dog Book.*
     New York: Howell, 1997.
Arden, Darlene. *The Angell Memorial Hospital Book of Wellness and Preventive Care for Dogs.* New York, NY: Contemporary Books, 2003.
Arden, Darlene. *Rover Get Off Her Leg.*
     Deerfield Beach, FL: Health Communications, Inc., 2007.
Arden, Darlene. *The Irrepressible Toy Dog.* New York: Howell Book House, 1998.

Baer, Ted. *Communicating with Your Dog,* 2nd ed. Hauppauge, NY: Barron's Educational Series, Inc., 1999.

Benning, Lee Edwards. *The Pet Profiteers.* New York: Quadrangle/The New York Times Book Co., 1976.

Bonham, Margaret H. *Introduction to Dog Agility,* 2nd ed. Hauppauge, NY: Barron's Educational Series, Inc., 2009.

Campbell, William E. *Behavior Problems in Dogs.* Goleta, CA: American Veterinary Publications, Inc., 1992.

Coile, D. Caroline. *Encyclopedia of Dog Breeds,* 2nd ed. Hauppauge, NY: Barron's Educational Series, Inc., 2005.

Coile, D. Caroline. *Show Me!,* 2nd ed. Hauppauge, NY: Barron's Educational Series, Inc., 1997.

Hope, Jerry. *The Breeders Guide to Raising Superstar Dogs.* Milner, GA: Diamond H, 2008.

Jones, Arthur F., and B. Hamilton. *The World Encyclopedia of Dogs.* NY: Galahad Books, 1971.

Mill, Charles E., Jr. "How Safe Is Air Travel for Dogs," *American Kennel Gazette,* Dec. 19, 1992, p. 71.

Smith, Cheryl S. *The Complete Guide to Showing Your Dog,* Roseville, CA: Prima Publishing, April 2001.

Walkowicz, Chris, and Bonnie Wilcox. *The Atlas of Dog Breeds of the World,* Neptune City, NJ: T.F.H., 1989.

Ward, Amy, DVM. *Small Animal Health Care: A Primer for Veterinary Clients.* Edwardsville, KS: Veterinary Medicine Publishing Co., 1983.

Weitzman, Nan, and Becker Ross. *The Dog Food Book.* Charleston, SC: Good Dog!, 1998.

About the Author

Susan Bulanda is a Pennsylvania-based dog behaviorist and trainer who has written and lectured extensively on canine topics. She is an award-winning author of *The Canine Source Book, Ready: A Step-by-Step Guide for Training the Search and Rescue Dog, Ready to Serve: Ready to Save-Strategies of Real-Life Search and Rescue Missions, God's Creatures: A Biblical View of Animals,* and *Faithful Friends: Holocaust Survivors Stories of the Pets Who Gave Them Comfort, Suffered Alongside Them, and Waited for Their Return.*

Cover Credits

Shutterstock: front cover, back cover, inside front cover, inside back cover.

Important Note

This pet owner's manual tells the reader how to buy or adopt and care for a Boston Terrier. The author and publisher consider it important to point out that the advice given in this book is meant primarily for normally developed dogs of excellent physical health and good character.

Anyone who adopts a fully grown dog should be aware that the animal has already formed its basic impressions of humans. The new owner should watch the dog carefully, including its behavior toward humans, and should meet the previous owner.

Caution is further advised in the association of children with dogs, in meeting with other dogs, and in exercising the dog without proper safeguards.

Even well-behaved and carefully supervised dogs sometimes do damage to someone else's property or cause accidents. It is therefore in the owner's interest to be adequately insured against such eventualities, and we strongly urge all dog owners to purchase a liability policy that covers their dog(s).

Photo Credits

Barbara Augello: pages 9, 23; DrsFosterSmith.com: pages 30, 40, 42; Carolyn Evans: page 27; Sharon Eide Elizabeth Flynn: pages 7, 12, 26, 45, 52, 66, 72, 87; iStock: pages 14, 84, 88; Daniel Johnson/Paulette Johnson: pages 48, 50 (top), 50 (bottom), 51, 53, 67, 68, 76, 91; Paulette Johnson: pages 15 (top), 16, 24, 46, 55, 56, 60, 69, 70, 71; Liz Kaye Photography: page 17; Oh My Dog! Photography: pages 5, 13, 21, 34, 43; Paws On The Run: page 33; Shutterstock: pages 2, 4, 25, 28, 29, 49, 57, 59, 62, 73, 77, 79, 80, 92, 93; SmartPakCanine.com: pages 10, 32, 35, 58, 75; Kira Stackhouse: pages 8, 15 (bottom), 19, 20, 31, 37, 65, 78, 81, 83; Connie Summers: page 39; Angie Wojciechowska: pages 89, 90.

© Copyright 2012, 2002, 1994 by Barron's Educational Series, Inc.

All inquiries should be addressed to:
Barron's Educational Series, Inc.
250 Wireless Boulevard
Hauppauge, NY 11788
www.barronseduc.com

Library of Congress Catalog Card No. 2011023842

ISBN-13: 978-0-7641-4747-0

Library of Congress Cataloging-in-Publication Data
Bulanda, Susan.
Boston terriers: everything about purchase, care, behavior, and training / Susan Bulanda. —3rd ed.
p. cm.
Includes bibliographical references and index.
ISBN 978-0-7641-4747-0
1. Boston terrier. I. Title.
SF429.B7B85 2012
636.72—dc23   2011023842

Printed in China
9 8 7 6 5 4 3 2 1